Kay Walter and Rüdiger Liedtke

111 Pla
in Brussels
That You
Shouldn't Miss

D1561870

(111)

emons:

© Emons Verlag GmbH
All rights reserved
All photos © Rüdiger Liedtke, apart from chapter 75 (NATO Headquarters
Brussels) and chapter 80 (Kay Walter). Image chapter 103: Jacques-Louis David,
The Death of Marat, 1793, Musée Royaux des Beaux Arts de Belgique.
Image chapter 90: Retabel van Pailhe, Antwerp, circa. 1510–1530,
Musée du Cinquantenaire.
Cover motif: fotolia.com/nui7711
Edited by Ros Horton
Design: Eva Kraskes, based on a design
by Lübbeke | Naumann | Thoben
Maps: altancicek.design, www.altancicek.de
Printing und binding: Lensing Druck GmbH & Co. KG,
Feldbachacker 16, 44149 Dortmund
Printed in Germany 2018
ISBN 978-3-7408-0259-2

Did you enjoy it? Do you want more?
Join us in uncovering new places around the world on:
www.111places.com

Foreword

Brussels, the capital of Belgium, is a complex city, a metropolis full of contradictions, structural fractures and surprises, and one that has had an eventful history through all the eras. Did you know that Albert Einstein and Marie Curie wrote physics history in the Hotel Metropole? That the foundations of the Communist Manifesto were laid down in Brussels? And that it is home to visible delusions of grandeur?

The people of Brussels are fun loving and open. There are extravagant restaurants, but also the best pommes frites in the world, unique chocolatiers and pubs. Brussels is the city of 1,000 types of beer, and home to a huge party and live music scene. It is shaped by the Middle Ages, but equally by Art Nouveau. Brussels has the most modern of museums, a diverse theatre landscape and is the world capital of the comic to boot.

But Brussels is also the headquarters of various European Union institutions, such as the European Commission, the Council of the European Union, and the European Parliament, as well as NATO. It's an internationally oriented city, a melting pot of nationalities. But just behind the dazzling façades of the EU is the African neighbourhood of Matongé, in which Belgium's colonial legacy lives on, still far from being adequately addressed. Then there's the district of Molenbeek, dominated by immigrant Moroccans and other North Africans and a heartland of Islam; it became infamous around the world as the home of those involved in the Paris attacks in 2015.

This all comes together to form a seemingly anarchic and difficult to govern city, which is also bilingual for good measure, with French and Flemish. But above all it is a city in which visitors can always make new and surprising discoveries.

111 Places in Brussels That You Shouldn't Miss is the slightly alternative travel guide through one of the most exciting and eclectic cities in Europe.

111 Places

1 A la Mort Subite

The ultimate beers – Gueuze, Kriek and Framboise

The Vossen family have run this listed tavern at the back exit of Galeries Saint-Hubert for four generations since 1928. Since then, neither the name nor the Art Nouveau decoration has changed, while the menu also continues to be limited to small snacks: omelettes, salads and cheeses. Nonetheless, the pub is still an absolute must for fans of Belgian beer. Of course, the fruit beers Kriek and Framboise – cherry and raspberry – are highly recommended, even if real ale purists won't hear of it. Likewise, strong abbey and Trappist beers, both bottled as well as on draught, are available at the bar.

But the real specialities here are the house-brewed Lambic and Gueuze, both types of beer that are produced by spontaneous fermentation. For outsiders, the sour taste takes some getting used to. Fans, on the other hand, make pilgrimages here, as these beers are unrivalled throughout the world. They are produced without the use of cultured yeast, using only the natural yeasts that float freely in the Brussels air. After fermentation, the beer is sealed, like Champagne, with a cork and stored in its bottle for two years. When the bottle is finally opened, it produces just the same satisfying sound as the popping of a Champagne bottle. Beware: Gueuze is considered a strong diuretic – the basis of a nice running gag in Asterix in Belgium.

The martial name A la Mort Subite – sudden death – has nothing to do with the effect of the beer, but rather a way to resolve a game of dice. Théophile Vossen's first pub, just like this one, was in the Belgian capital's banking district. If the bankers' lunch break ended before a round had finished, it would be decided on a single throw of the dice, the Mort Subite. The name stuck, for both the beer and the pub. Just to the right of the door is a photo of a former regular: Jacques Brel often liked to sit and drink here.

Address Rue Montagne aux Herbes Potagères / Warmoesberg 7, 1000 Brussels, +32 (0)2 5131318, www.alamortsubite.com/en | **Getting there** Bus 29, 38, 63, 66 or 86 to Arenberg or Assaut | **Hours** Daily 11–1am | **Tip** At Rue des Alexiens 55, slightly off the beaten track for those from out of town, you will find La Fleur en Papier Doré (The Gold-Paper Flower), a Brussels institution and a former local for many artists including René Magritte.

2 __ The ADAM

A shrine to plastic

The musical *Hair* begins with the 1960s' hymn 'The Age of Aquarius'. However, that decade may have been more appropriately characterised as the age of plastic. The first piece of furniture made completely out of plastic was produced in 1960, but the oil-based material quickly went out of fashion after the first oil crisis in 1973. In between was a frenzy of colours, in bold yet affordable designs, and the advent of a whole generation, whose clothes were, to a great extent, made out of plastic.

The new Art & Design Atomium Museum (ADAM) is dedicated to this period – the only one of its kind. It is an ode to pop culture, a multicolour orgy with television sets, telephones and record players; ball chairs, open and closable; desks, lamps and art objects; blow-up and fibreglass armchairs; as well as parts of a discotheque from an Italian hotel. Here the swinging sixties celebrates its resurrection. Philippe Decelle has been collecting these objects (including pieces by designers such as Joe Colombo, Günther Beltzig and Verner Panton) since 1986 and has now donated them to the museum. Interest in the collection was expressed from both London and New York, but Philippe Decelle endowed his hometown, in particular because of the location here, right next to Atomium, another symbol of the new dawn. Decelle thought they fitted well together, especially as there was a similar, but much smaller collection in one of the Atomium's spheres. This is now integrated into ADAM.

ADAM opened in December 2015 with the so-called Plasticarium as its centrepiece and permanent exhibition. Films, from Alain Resnais to Andy Warhol, from *Barbarella* to *The Graduate*, all help to make the epoch come to life. The collection is also extended into the present, with pieces by renowned artists such as Philippe Starck and Charles Kaisin as well as special exhibitions on various themes to do with modern design.

Address Place de Belgique/Belgiëplein 1, 1020 Brussels (Laeken/Laken), +32 (0)2 4754764, www.adamuseum.be | Getting there Metro 6, tram 7 or bus 84 or 88 to Heysel/Heizel | Hours Daily 10am–6pm | Tip The impressive Church of Our Lady of Laeken (Parvis Notre-Dame), built by Joseph Poelaert in a Neo-Gothic style with a 99-metre-high steeple, was consecrated in 1872. Members of the royal family are buried in the crypt here.

3 _ The Africa Museum

The deceptive veneer of a dark colonial history

Belgium and the Congo are inextricably linked by a very brutal colonial history, which Belgium has to thank for a large part of its wealth. The former colony is now splintered into several states, which hit the headlines time and again with bloody wars over diamonds and 'rare earth'. The majority of Belgians only really began to recognise this in 2000, when the then Prime Minister Guy Verhofstadt apologised several times for the historical crimes his country had committed.

The Africa Museum in the suburbs of Tervuren is closely related to this history. The 1896 building became the 'Royal Museum for Central Africa' in 1910. King Leopold II had financed the construction of the castle-like property solely from income from Africa. The 'Congo Free State' – officially proclaimed in 1897 – was the private property of the king from 1885 to 1908 and provided huge profits from trade in rubber and diamonds. Black Africans were not allowed to enter Belgium for the following 50 years. It wasn't until 1958 that some African families were brought to the country and presented in the museum as 'exhibition pieces' during the World's Fair.

In 2005, an exhibition on the colonial past was created in collaboration with Congolese academics. The themes covered were trade, administration, mission work and cottage industries, but not the suppression of the Congolese under Belgian rule. The museum closed in December 2013 and is due to reopen in mid-2018 with a new concept and new buildings by the architect Stéphane Beel. Then it must surely be time to address Leopold II's personal involvement in the Congo and Belgium's role in the murder of the first freely elected president of the Congo, Patrice Lumumba (1925–1961). The previous representation of Belgium's colonial history was more than questionable. A new, contemporary presentation is absolutely crucial for a museum of this kind.

Address Leuvensesteenweg 13, 3080 Tervuren, +32 (0)2 7695211, www.africamuseum.be |
Getting there Metro 1 to Montgomery, then S 44 to Terminus | Hours The museum is due
to reopen in June 2018. | Tip Just in front of the museum, a stone elephant, ridden by three
naked Africans, makes manifest the old museum's prettified image of Africa. Albéric Collin
created the sculpture in 1935 at the behest of the chocolate factory Côte d'Or, who have an
elephant in their logo.

4 The Alleyway

The old-town alleyways that close for the night

Medieval Brussels was one of the most beautiful cities in Europe. This Brussels, however, was burnt to the ground, completely and repeatedly. Don't let anyone tell you there are still large parts of it standing. Even the Grand-Place was almost completely destroyed by French bombardment on 13 and 14 August, 1695. It was only after its reconstruction that it acquired the complete baroque façade that it still has today. But there are a couple of indications as to how the old centre, from Grand-Place to Sainte-Cathérine and Beguinage, may once have looked. House façades are not so useful as clues, but the course of streets is.

And some of them are clearly from the time before motorised traffic: alleyways, narrow even for pedestrians and definitely too tight for cars. Some things, which at first look like the entrance to a house, are in fact streets or impasses, which can mean both narrow passage as well as dead end. Impasse Schuddeveld, for example, is a cul-de-sac that leads straight to Théâtre Toone's bar. Impasse Ossen on the other hand leads to several residential houses. Most people accidently walk past Impasse Cadeaux / Geschenkengang – apart from those who know this is the way to the pub L'Imaige Nostre-Dame. The same can be said of Impasse Saint-Nicolas, which leads to Au Bon Vieux Temps. Those who don't know any better assume the two small arches with the decorative statues and houses built over them are front doors. In fact, they are old-town alleyways, which have doors that still close them off during the night. This is also true of Rue de la Machoire / Kinnebak, which branches off from Rue de Flandre. Rue Du Chien Marin / Zeehondstraat and Rue du Nom de Jésus, a few steps further, which lead to the Fish Market, are also worth a visit. Probably the most beautiful and romantic of all the alleyways, though, is Rue de la Cigogne / Ooievaarstraat – 'stork street'.

Address Rue de la Cigogne/Ooievaarstraat, 1000 Brussels | Getting there Pedestrian
zone best reached from Bourse | Hours Always during the day | Tip A chapter of Brussels'
medieval monastic history can be viewed under the asphalt right next to the Bourse. The
museum Bruxella 1238 has presented the remains of the Gothic chancels of the monastic
church of the Minorites as well as the brick burial chambers since 1993 (Rue de la
Bourse/Beursstraat, +34 (0)2 2794371; guided tours: first Wednesday of the month).

5___Atelier de Moulage
Classic plaster

Most locals will have heard of 'their' plaster cast atelier, but only few will have visited it. That's a real shame, and not only because it is one of the last institutions of its kind. The atelier is somewhat hidden underneath the Museum of Art and History, but can be viewed without paying an entrance fee. Originally it even comprised its own museum for plaster sculptures and reliefs. Such collections of plaster casts were quite common up into the 19th century. Otherwise you would only ever have been able to admire Michelangelo's *David* in its original form in Florence. In the time before film and photography, plaster casts were produced and then exhibited in museums around the world.

A good 16,000 hollow casts are stored in Atelier de Moulage: from the Palaeolithic *Venus of Willendorf,* an 11-centimetre-tall statuette (for 80 years after it was found in 1908 it was considered so precious that there was basically only one copy that could be exhibited), via busts of Danton, Robespierre or Beethoven to Michelangelo's *David* in its original size of five metres. A plaster statue of that size is, like most statues, put together from several partial casts.

The atelier has an inventory of over 4,000 effigies in total – from the Stone Age to the 18th century. The artists who work here are happy to talk about their work and show you the huge warehouse. All of the casts are sold here on site, not only to museum shops around the world, but also to individual customers, who place the statues in their gardens or the busts on their mantelpieces. There is even a comprehensive catalogue. This is where the Brussels City Museum orders its statues of *Manneken Pis* for his ever-changing wardrobe of clothes, and where art schools buy Moulage articles as teaching materials and style tests. The American artist Jeff Koons also ordered his *David* here, before reworking it himself.

Address Parc du Cinquantenaire/Jubelpark 10, 1000 Brussels, +32 (0)2 7417294 | Getting there Metro 1 or tram 81 to Merode or bus 22, 27 or 80 to Gaulois | Hours Tue–Fri 9.30am–noon & 1.30–4pm | Tip Above the atelier is AutoWorld. Alongside the Cadillac Cabriolet that drove John F. Kennedy through Berlin, it has everything from the Ford T1 to modern sports cars.

6 The Aviation Hall

One of a kind in Europe

Part of a gigantic historic museum complex, the hall, with its numerous glass domes and towers, exceeds all dimensions, and what it contains is unmatched anywhere else in Europe. Aircraft as far as the eye can see. The very beginnings of aviation are represented with Belgian inventor César Battaille's triplane from 1911. There's hardly a model missing in the rows of exhibits from the World War I period, with Aviatik, Nieuport 23 and Fieseler Storch. The only original surviving Nieuport 17 C1 is here in Brussels. World War II is also well represented with many aeroplanes such as the British Hurricane and Spitfire and a Belgian F-16. And then there's the jet age, with international military aviation engineering, from the US-American Phantom to the Soviet MIG 23. A Caravelle from the early Belgian airline company Sabena flies above them all – just one of the numerous passenger and freight aircraft from various technological periods presented to the visitor in an exciting way. You can even climb into a fighter plane yourself.

The aviation exhibition is part of the Royal Museum of the Armed Forces and Military History, which also includes large halls containing cannons and tanks, flags and uniforms. There are historic collections from all the eras of Belgian military history, from the Austrian Netherlands, the Dutch period, the Napoleon era up to the Belgian Revolution. Another part of the exhibition is dedicated to the occupation of Belgium by the German Wehrmacht in World War II.

The military museum was founded in 1911 and is based on a comprehensive collection of militaria that was compiled for the World Fair in 1910, in order to fittingly present the glory of Belgium. It was eventually opened right next to the triumphal arch at Jubelpark in 1923. The aviation exhibition, with more than 130 historical aeroplanes, has existed since 1972.

Address Musée Royal de l'Armée et d'Histoire Militaire / Koninklijk Museum van het Leger en de Krijgsgeschiedenis, Parc du Cinquantenaire / Jubelpark 3, 1000 Brussels, +32 (0)2 7377811, www.klm-mra.be | **Getting there** Metro 1 or 5, tram 80 or bus 27, 28, 36, 61, 67 or 80 to Schuman or Merode | **Hours** Tue – Sun 9am – 5pm | **Tip** It's worth taking a look at the extensive murals on the open, column-ornamented circular buildings on both sides of the triumphal arch.

7　Bains d'Ixelles

Swimming in an Art Nouveau ambience

In Rue de la Natation / Zwemkunststraat you will find the oldest indoor swimming baths in the Brussels region, built in 1904 as the public baths for Ixelles / Elsene – though you may be forgiven for walking straight past. Just trust in the house number – you would never guess from the outside that a swimming pool is hidden behind these doors. Any possible confusion is forgotten once you are inside what is, by today's standards, a very special baths. The fin de siècle industrial architecture with visible steel girders and a self-supporting roof, partly made of glass, is hugely impressive. And then there's the pool with its decidedly unusual dimensions – not in accordance with competition standards – of 29.2 by 14.4 metres at a depth of 3.25 metres and a water temperature of 28 degrees. The water polo section of the 'Royal Swimming Club of Ixelles 1904' is famous.

Today the Bains d'Ixelles is a listed building, not because of its age, but rather because of its changing facilities. Here, rather than collective changing rooms separated into male and female areas, there are countless individual cubicles, rather like small beach huts – all in the style of the era. Organised in blocks, they encircle the whole pool across two storeys and thus lend the hall a very special appearance. You simply enter an empty cubicle, get changed and leave your clothes there. Bathing caps are obligatory, but can be borrowed.

At the beginning of the 20th century, halls like this one were built in several districts of Brussels, many of which were still independent authorities at the time, especially in the working-class areas. There were social, but in particular hygiene reasons for this: very few apartments had bathrooms. Only two of them are preserved, renovated and still in operation: Bains d'Ixelles and Piscine Victor Boin, built in 1905, in the neighbouring district of Saint-Gilles.

Address Bains d'Ixelles, Rue de la Natation / Zwemkunststraat 10, 1050 Brussels (Ixelles / Elsene), +32 (0)2 5156931 | **Getting there** Tram 81 to Germoir, bus 59 to Natation or bus 60 to Blyckaert | **Hours** Mon 8am–9pm, Tue–Sun 8am–6pm | **Tip** Piscine Victor Boin at Rue de la Perche 38 from 1905 is designed in a very similar way and even has three storeys of changing cubicles.

8__ The Basilica

For many locals, it's just plain ugly

As we all know, beauty is in the eye of the beholder – and you certainly won't be able to avoid beholding the National Basilica of the Sacred Heart. The sacred building sits atop the Koekelberg and is clearly visible from almost any point in the city. But only when you get closer to the church – whether by foot, car or tram – do you begin to appreciate how big it really is. At 141 metres long, 107 metres wide and 93 metres tall, it is the fifth biggest church in the world and the largest Art Deco building by a long way. Fifty-three metres up is a viewing platform with what must be the best view of the city. When the weather is fine the view extends to Flanders and Pajottenland, sometimes all the way to Mechelen.

In 1905, the 75th anniversary of the state of Belgium, King Leopold II awarded the commission to build a Neo-Gothic cathedral. The construction of the colossus was interrupted by World War I, among other things, and first resumed in 1920 under the architect Albert van Huffel (1877 – 1935), now with an Art Deco design. Its optical simplicity was supposed to cut costs. The church was consecrated in 1951, Pope Pius XII conferred it the title Basilica Minor in 1952, but the National Basilica wasn't really finished until the end of 1970, 65 years after construction began. Today, the church offers a changing programme of art exhibitions and is home to two museums: one for modern religious art and the second on the work of the Order of the Black Sisters. The Belgian national holiday on 21 July begins with a Te Deum to the royal family. For a long time this state occasion took place in the Basilica, but now only in special cases.

The National Basilica is imposing, true to the period, and a symbol of the Belgian state and faith. One thing it certainly isn't to these eyes is beautiful. Van Huffel's late Art Deco style is all too reminiscent of fascist architecture.

Address Parvis de la Basilique / Basiliekvoorplein 1, 1083 Brussels (Ganshoren), +32 (0)2 4211667, www.basilicakoekelberg.be | Getting there Metro 2 or 6 to Simonis, then tram 19 to Boessart-Basilique or bus 87, 212, 213 or 214 to Collège du Sacré-Cœur; free car park | Hours Summer 9am–5pm, winter 10am–4pm | Tip The cemetery in the neighbouring district of Laeken is small, but locals call it 'our Père Lachaise' nonetheless. *The Thinker* by Auguste Rodin is to be found near the entrance, not a copy but in fact an original statue.

9 The Battlefield
The historical setting of Waterloo

On 18 June, 1815, a battle raged on the hills near Waterloo to the south of Brussels that was to change the face and history of Europe. The Allied army led by the British Duke of Wellington (1769–1852) and the Prussian army allied with him crushed Napoleon's army and paved the way for the French Emperor's 'Waterloo'. The 'Hundred Days', his second period of imperial rule, ended just four days later. Napoleon was forced to abdicate and was exiled to Saint Helena. The battle, in which 45,000 died, was one of the most brutal massacres in human history. The dead and injured, people and animals, lay piled up on top of each other, to a depth of three metres in places. Napoleon had promised his generals a certain victory on the morning of 18 June. By the evening, a third of all the men who went into battle were dead.

The modern Museum Le Mémorial, directly below the former battlefield and not visible from the outside, was inaugurated on the 200th anniversary of the battle in 2015. The museum makes good use of the possibilities of cutting-edge multimedia presentation. Visitors can have the historical context of events leading up to Waterloo explained to them and even go into battle with each or any of the armies involved. A thrilling 4-D film by the Belgian director Gérard Corbiau will give an impression of how soldiers may have actually experienced the battle, while the whole thing is also re-enacted in the flesh by hundreds of amateur actors every year on a weekend around 18 June.

The rotunda with its legendary battle panorama is from 1912 – at the time it was the most modern way to make history come alive. Next to it is the manmade Lion Mound with views across the historic terrain. In addition, there is the Wellington Museum, also designed in 2015, which presents a direct comparison of the life journeys of Napoleon and Wellington.

Within the image (map relief labels):

OFFERT PAR LE WATERLOO COMMITTEE
ET WATERLOO - RELAIS DE L'HISTOIRE

NAPOLEON

GARDE IMPERIALE

PLANCENOIT

KELLERMANN

LOBAU

BELLE-
ALLIANCE

REILLE

MILHAUD

GOUMONT

DROUET J'ERLON

HAIE-
SAINTE

LION / ORANGE

19H   PIRCH

PRINCE

FICHERMONT

HILL

KULOW

PAPELOTTE

PICTON

UXBRIDGE

17H

BLUCHER

MONT S. JEAN

BRAINE - L'ALLEUD

ZIETEN

WELLINGTON

20H

Address Route du Lion, 1420 Braine l'Alleud, +32 (0)2 3851912 | Getting there Bus
(from Gare du Midi / Zuidstation) Line W and Line 365(a) | Hours Apr–Sept
9.30am–6.30pm, Oct–Mar 10am–6pm | Tip As you are beyond the gates of the city, why
not visit the massive ruins of the Cistercian Abbey of Villers, established in 1146 (Abbaye
de Villers-la-Ville, Rue de l'Abbaye 55, 1495 Villers-la-Ville). There is a restaurant in the
former monastery mill and a small brewery next door.

10__ The Bavarian Mission

Fairy-tale castle in the European quarter

The Bavarian state government maintains a special relationship with the European capital of Brussels: in Bavaria, they like to complain about 'EU bureaucrats' but in Brussels, on the other hand, no other German state has such a finely spun network of relationships at its disposal. In the centre of this web is the Bavarian state mission, officially a department of the state chancellery. It is the most luxurious and by far the grandest of all the German state missions, which meant it hit the headlines even before it opened. It's located in Parc Léopold, in the heart of the European quarter, right next to the EU Parliament, in what was formerly Institut Pasteur. The castle-like premises from 1903 are made up of three buildings: institute, villa and stables. The Nobel Prize-winner Jules Bordet (1870–1961) lived and researched immunology and bacteriology here. The institute existed until 1987. Afterwards the building fell into disrepair. The reason: property speculation, ubiquitous in the EU quarter even back then. In 2001, the Free State of Bavaria bought the 'prime plot', as we now know, for the bargain price of 29.4 million euros, and elaborately renovated the three buildings true to style. It thus saved the complex from doom while providing itself with classy representation.

Brussels gossiped about the Bavarians and their grand 'palatial' statement, especially the representatives of other German states. Today, we know that almost all of their state missions were more expensive. Reinhold Bocklet, the former Bavarian MEP, had a sound nose for a good deal and as well as the right contacts, as the vice president of the Committee of the Regions. The mayor of Brussels certainly gave express thanks for the preservation of the Institut Pasteur at the opening. Alongside representative rooms, the mission is also home to a bar and an events hall in the former stables.

Address Rue Wiertz 77, 1000 Brussels, +32 (0)2 2374811 | Getting there Metro 2 or 6 to Trone / Troon or bus 21 or 27 to Parc Léopold | Hours During events or by arrangement | Tip The former racecourse at Boitsfort (today Brussels Golf Club) with its historic grandstands is certainly worth a visit (Chaussée de la Hulpe 53).

11__The Beguinage
Church, nursing home and place of reflection

It is only a hop, skip and jump from the hectic city centre to the beguinage north of the fish market, but here you will be immersed immediately in an oasis of peace and reflection. Here on the small square behind the baroque church of Saint-Jean-Baptiste au Béguinage, which was laid out in front of the old beguinage, you are likely to encounter very few people, perhaps a couple of boule players.

The Hospice Pachéco nursing home was built in 1824 on the site of the beguinage. This is turn had been founded in 1250 as the home of the Brussels Beguines, a Catholic women's movement predominantly native to Belgian Flanders and The Netherlands. Over 1,200 sisters lived in this 'temporary convent' – the Beguines lived somewhere between strict monastic rule and a layperson's life – at the end of the 13th century. Alongside the central buildings and residential houses, their estate included a hospital, a mill on the Senne/Zenne as well as assembly rooms – all laid out around a square with a church. A city within the city, sealed off to the outside world, with numerous privileges. That's precisely why the Beguines were a thorn in the side of rulers and, time and again, the clergy. At times, they were accused of heresy, though they were comparatively liberal-minded, then they were attacked on accusations of tax exemption and finally ransacked after the reformation. In the course of the French Revolution and rampant anti-clerical policies, the Brussels beguinage was closed in 1797/98.

A church stood in the centre of the beguinage. Initially it was a chapel, then a triple-nave Gothic basilica, which was plundered in 1578 by the Calvinists and later destroyed. The Flemish-Italian baroque building of Saint-Jean-Baptiste au Béguinage was erected on its foundations from 1657 on, built to the plans of the Brabant architect Lucas Faydherbe (1617–1697).

Address Place du Béguinage / Begijnhof, 1000 Brussels | **Getting there** Metro 3 or 4 to De Brouckère, metro 1, 5 to Sainte-Catherine / Sint-Katelijne or bus 88 to Begijnhof | **Hours** The square is accessible 24 hours; church Mon–Sat 10am–5pm, Sun 10am–8pm | **Tip** Porte de Hal / Hallepoort (Boulevard du Midi 150), the last meaningful symbol of Brussels' second medieval fortifications and built between 1356 and 1383, is worth a visit. It is also home to the Museum of Medieval City History.

12 The Brel House

For fans and those who wish to be

Only a stone's throw away from the Grand-Place is the small square Vieille Halle aux Blés / Oud Korenhuis. Jacques Brel, Brussels' most famous son, is commemorated at house number 11. Amsterdam, Ne me quitte pas, Marieke, Le plat pays, Le Moribond (better known as 'Seasons in the Sun') – there can't be many people who haven't heard at least one of his songs. To this day 250,000 records of his chansons are sold every year. But Brussels and the Belgians haven't always been proud of him. He made too much fun of the petit bourgeois, branded the nationalistic Flemings as Nazis or caricatured the Brussels dialect, as many thought. Brel himself had always stressed that he loved the dialect, and sang of it as 'my flat country'.

Jacques Romain Georges Brel was born at Avenue du Diamant 138 in Brussels-Schaerbeek on 8 April, 1929. There was nothing to suggest that the youngest son of a cardboard manufacturer would one day become 'Grand Jacques', the famous chanson singer. Little Jacky was a bad pupil and had to repeat several years. He was only really interested in the theatre, his scout group and music. In the end he was taken out of school in order to work in his father's factory. After such a miserable childhood, the prospect of a life following a preordained petit bourgeois path tipped him over the edge. At the age of 24, Brel was already married and father of two daughters, but he ran away in order to seek his fortune in Paris as a singer. It took some time. It was with 'Quand on n'a que l'amour' ('When love is all you have') that he finally achieved the breakthrough in 1956. The following 10 years were a victory march – the man with the horsey face and the big hands became a celebrated star. Brel's career as a performer ended on 16 May, 1967 with a last concert in Roubaix. In 1978 he had to cancel a world circumnavigation and soon after died of lung cancer.

Address Place de Vieille Halle aux Blés/Oud Korenhuis 11, 1000 Brussels, +32 (0)2 5111020, www.jacquesbrel.be | Getting there Metro 1 or 5 to Gare Centrale/Centraal Station or bus 48 or 95 to Parlement Bruxellois | Hours Tue–Sat noon–6pm, Sun too in summer | Tip The museum offers an audio tour that leads visitors through the city centre with stories and anecdotes by and about Jacques Brel (and of course some of his chansons).

13__ The Brewery
Delicacies of spontaneous fermentation

It is only to be found in Brussels, in the Senne valley, and Anderlecht is a hotspot. The particles of wild yeast floating around in the air make the beer ferment spontaneously, leading to the production, following a traditional process, i.e. without the addition of any other kind of yeast, of so-called lambic. It is brewed from the middle of October to the start of April – the rest of the year is generally too warm and would allow the influence of other, undesired fungi. The fermentation process is in fact a highly hygienic one. The Cantillon is the last brewery in Brussels that produces in this way, according to a process that was used by all 100 of the city's breweries until the discovery of bacteria and thus yeast by Louis Pasteur in 1860. The extremely complicated fermentation of lambic in oak and chestnut wood barrels takes up to three years. Afterwards, various vintages of lambic are blended in to create a cuvée (or blend). This Gueuze is handled as carefully as a Champagne wine – an exclusive, flavourful, but quirky drink.

The brewery, founded in 1900 by Paul Cantillon in Anderlecht and now in its fourth generation of family ownership, has always brewed exclusively lambic beers.

As Cantillon's elaborate brewing process and the brewery's limited space do not allow for an increase in output, the family decided to set up a museum with tastings, in order to bring the specialities of spontaneously fermented Belgian beer, especially during the brewing-free months, to a wider audience and to generate additional income. There, you can also look over the brewers' shoulders while they are brewing lambic or are engaged in the elaborate process of searching through various lambic vintages for the right composition for gueuze, which then ferments further in the bottle and can be stored for many years. Or when they brew the fruity beers Kriek, Faro or Vigneronne.

Address Brasserie Cantillon, Rue Gheude 56, 1070 Brussels (Anderlecht), +32 (0)2 5214928, www.cantillon.be | Getting there Metro 3 or 4 to Gare du Midi/Zuidstation and Lemonnier or tram 81 to Place Bara/Baraplein | Hours Daily 10am–5pm, apart from Wed & Sun, last admission 4pm (ad hoc guided tours possible) | Tip The Belgian Brewers Museum is well worth seeing and affords a comprehensive insight into the craft of brewing (Grand-Place 10, +32 (0)2 5114987).

14 Bruegel's Grave
Notre-Dame de la Chapelle/Kapellekerk graveyard

During his years in Brussels, the famous Flemish painter Pieter Bruegel the Elder (around 1525–1569) created masterpieces such as *The Tower of Babel* (1563), *The Land of Cockaigne* (1567) and *The Peasant Wedding*. You can still find him at work on the square at the side of the Romanesque church Notre-Dame de la Chapelle, where the cemetery was once located. In a sculpture modelled in 2015 by Tom Frantzen, born in 1954 not far from Brussels, the medieval Bruegel is presented to the viewer, larger than life, in front of an abstract, visionary canvas, looking surprised, with palette and brush in hand. A small monkey is providing him with assistance from his shoulder.

Here, on the edge of the Marollen neighbourhood, not far from his home and workshop at Hoogstraat 132, the ingenious painter and his wife Maria Coecke, the daughter of his teacher, the artist Pieter Coecke van Aelst (1502–1550), lie buried, according to lore, in a side chapel of the Notre-Dame de la Chapelle. In fact, this is the very church in which the two of them married in 1563. On view today is a marble memorial plaque, created by Bruegel's son Jan, which was restored in 1667 by his great grandson. He decorated the epitaph with a painting by Peter Paul Rubens, a copy of which can be seen here today. The original of *Christ Giving the Keys to St Peter* was sold in 1765 and now hangs on the walls of the Gemäldegalerie in Berlin.

The Romanesque church from the 13th century was an early place of pilgrimage due to its various relics of the Holy Cross and was rebuilt predominantly in the style of Brabant Gothic after a fire. It also bears a second memorial plaque from the year 1834. This one refers to Frans Anneessens, also buried here in Notre-Dame de la Chapelle, who was sentenced to death and executed on Grand-Place in 1719 for being a fighter for Brussels' independence.

Address Notre-Dame de la Chapelle, Place de la Chapelle, 1000 Brussels | Getting there Metro 1 or 5 to Gare Centrale/Centraal Station or bus 27 or 48 to Chapelle | Hours Daily 10am–4pm | Tip The grimacing faces and water-spouting heads on the frieze of the south portal are worth taking a look at. Next door to the church, at Gare La Chapelle, is the biggest skatepark in Brussels.

15 _ Broadcasting House
Jazz and classical music of the very highest standard in Flagey

Flagey – as the locals call the square, the building and in fact the whole area – is a place for the young. Any time of the day is good for seeing and being seen in the hippest bars and cafés or hanging out on the grass around the two lakes, the Etangs d'Ixelles. The square is dominated by the former home of Belgian radio.

Yellow brick and glass in alternating stripes, rounded edges instead of corners, adorn both the building itself and its four-storey tower. Some compare the sight with the silhouette of a luxury liner, especially if you see it mirrored in the water. Designed in a modernist style in 1930 by Belgian architect Joseph Diongre (1878–1963), it went into operation in 1938 as one of the first radio buildings in the world and was home even then to several studios of various sizes and tonal characteristics for the live broadcast of concerts, symphonies or radio plays. Studio 4 became famous for its organ with 8,000 pipes and its outstanding acoustics. In 1953, Belgian television also moved in, broadcasting from here for 21 years. Then it got too cramped, the broadcasters moved out, and the building was converted into a cultural centre. But the house and in particular the technology fell prey to the ravages of time. The building, precious parts of the late Art Deco interior design, the technology and ultimately the square were elaborately renovated in several stages between 1997 and 2008.

Today, the five studios, especially number 4, are once again considered global leaders in terms of sound quality. The programme is full of exquisite concerts. The halls are home to the philharmonic orchestra and the Queen Elisabeth competition for young talents in classical music, the Brussels Jazz Festivals and the Flagey Piano Days. Several concerts in one evening is not an uncommon occurrence. There are also cinemas and the famous Café Belga on the ground floor.

Address Rue du Belvédère 27, 1050 Brussels (Ixelles / Elsene), +32 (0)2 6411010, www.flagey.be | Getting there Tram 81 or 83 or bus 38, 59, 60 or 71 to Flagey | Hours Ticket shop, Tue–Fri noon–5pm and one hour before events begin | Tip Frit Flagey has been a Brussels institution for decades and takes one of the top spots in the list of the most popular Fritkots.

16__The Canal
Waterway and city harbour

It is sometimes quite disconcerting when you encounter a huge cargo ship in the middle of Brussels, forcing its way tight up against the quay walls of the Charleroi–Brussels canal that traverses the narrow passages of the city. Brussels is dissected by the 74-kilometre canal, which connects Charleroi in the south of Belgium with the capital and merges into the Brussels–Scheldt canal to Antwerp at the northern end of the city. The west bank passes over to the city centre and to Schaerbeek; the east side forms the border to Anderlecht, Molenbeek and Laeken.

Plans for a waterway between Charleroi, the centre of the coal fields, and Brussels were already being made in the first half of the 16th century under Charles V. The canal, in its current structure, was opened in 1832, but regular expansion work followed due to the ever-growing size of the ships. Of the canal's 11 locks, 2 are in Brussels – in Anderlecht and Molenbeek.

A boat trip through Brussels is relatively unspectacular over long stretches, as the canal lies a few metres under the city's street level, mainly with built up side walls. But the same route presents itself very differently to pedestrians – on the east bank of the canal are the old brewing plants, among them the legendary Bellevue brewery. These now house hotels, museums and shops.

From Place Sainctelette, where the canal opens out into a broad basin, you come across large coloured paintings from the comic *Corto Maltese* by the Italian illustrator Hugo Pratt (1927–1995) on the outer walls of the warehouses.

A little piece of the Mediterranean is created right in front of this for six weeks a year, in the months of July and August. Tonnes of sand are dumped to form a long beach on which beach volleyball, bocce and beach football are played, and is accompanied by cocktail bars, music and film screenings.

Address Canal between Porte de Flandre / Vlaamsesteenweg and Place Sainctelette-Plein (Bassin Beco) as well as Place des Armateurs (transition to the industrial harbour Bassin Vergote), 1000 Brussels | Getting there Metro 1 or 5 to Comte de Flandre / Graaf van Vlaanderen, metro 2 or 6 to Yser / IJzer or bus 14, 15, 57 or 88 to Willebroek or Armateurs | Hours Accessible 24 hours | Tip You can enjoy a great view of the canal and the harbour from the terrace of the public, nostalgic looking clubhouse of the Royal Yacht Club in Chaussée de Vilvorde in Laeken (get there by car).

17 — The Carillon
The carillon on Mont des Arts

The mighty carillon hadn't been heard or even noticed by anyone at all for many years. It slowly weathered on the exterior façade of the Palais der Dynastie (today a depot of the Royal Library), built in 1964 by Belgian architect Jules Ghobert (1881–1973), rendered immobile with transmission damage. But the huge clockwork installation with its 14 bells has been running around the clock again since 2015, attracting the gaze of those at the foot of the Kunstberg, up above the street, where the Palais straddles it, forming a passage to the lower town. People stand before it in awe as a Walloon or a Flemish melody play alternately on the hour.

Twelve moving figures, sunk into the wall, around a gleaming gilded clock, which all together represent a piece of Brussels city history, adorn the wall and can be seen from all around. Below the coloured figures – including Godfrey of Bouillon from the 11th century; Emperor Charles V: the painter Peter Paul Rubens; the Count of Egmont, who was executed and beheaded on Grand-Place in 1568, with his head under his arm; and a soldier from World War I – each representing an hour, there are 11 bells hanging visibly above the archway. They were made in the legendary French bell foundry Paccard and represent the Belgian provinces, art and science. There are more bells sunk into the façade's alcoves and hidden behind each of the figures.

But the most spectacular bell sits above the carillon to the right, protruding a little from the roof of the building. The sight of the 2.8-metre-tall figure, dressed in the fashion of the year of revolution 1830, hitting the biggest bell, the 1,750-kilogramme tenor bell, with a hammer on the hour, is visible from far and wide. The so-called *Jacquemart*, a sculpture by the artist Henri Albada (1907–2000), born in the municipality Uccle in 1907, represents the citizens of Brussels.

Address Mont des Arts/Kunstberg, 1000 Brussels | Getting there Metro 1 or 5 to Gare Centrale/Centraal Station | Hours Accessible 24 hours | Tip There is another carillon on the roof of the parliament building at Rue de Louvain/Leuvenseweg 13.

18_ The Cemetery

The Cimetière du Dieweg and its celebrities

The attraction of this cemetery is its enchanted nature, offering the visitor a voyage of discovery of a special kind. You don't need to have a predilection for cemeteries, but what you will encounter here is unusual. The cemetery is completely overgrown, some of the graves overrun by plants, the gravestones broken and crestfallen, as if an earthquake had struck. Elsewhere the gravestones are sunk into the ground and you have to take care that you don't fall down a hole yourself. Is all this really intentional? The minimal upkeep does have its attraction. All that the two cemetery gardeners – also quite bizarre characters – ensure is that there is no vandalism and that plant life doesn't gain the upper hand on the graves, some of which are unusual and worth seeing. Among all the apparent chaos there are numerous people and important families buried here who have made their mark on the city and written history, particularly during the 19th century.

The cemetery was established in 1866 in order to take in victims of a cholera epidemic, when several other cemeteries closed simultaneously after reaching capacity. Ten years later, after the closure of the cemetery of Saint-Gilles, it also became a cemetery of the Brussels Jewish community. Imposing tombs of notable Jewish banking dynasties can be found in the rear part of the cemetery. The numerous Art Nouveau graves, such as that of the architect Paul Hankar, also stand out. Others were designed by Victor Horta.

When the cemetery finally became too small and a bigger one opened in nearby Verrewinkel in 1945, the cemetery on Dieweg closed in 1958. Only in a very few exceptional cases are people still buried here. The most prominent 'Dieweger' is the cartoonist and *Tintin* illustrator Hergé, who was buried here in 1983. The cemetery on Dieweg has been officially listed since 1997.

Address Cimetière du Dieweg, Dieweg 95, 1180 Brussels (Uccle/Ukkel) | **Getting there** Tram 92 or 97 to Dieweg or bus 60 to Chênaie | **Hours** Tue – Fri 9.30am – noon & 1.30 – 4pm; guided tours must be requested (+32 (0)2 3741750) | **Tip** Musée David et Alice van Buuren (Uccle, Avenue Léo Errera 41), an Art Deco villa with an astonishing art collection and a fantastic garden, is definitely worth a visit. And the impressive Uccle observatory is not far away either.

19 The Chalet Robinson

An island in the middle of the city

The large deciduous Forêt de Soignes / Zoniënwoud extends from the south, right into the city centre of Brussels like a wedge, with its tip, the Bois de la Cambre / Terkamerenbos, at the southern end of Boulevard Louise. The landscaped park was designed in 1861, in the English style, by the now largely unknown Belgian German landscape architect Friedrich Eduard Keilig (1827–1895), who was heavily involved in the development of Brussels as a green city. He also built the parks of Laeken, Saint-Gilles and Forest, the racecourse at Boitsfort as well as the Etangs d'Ixelles. But Forêt des Soignes, and in particular Bois de la Cambre, are the ultimate daytrip destinations in Brussels. At weekends the roads in the forest are mostly closed to traffic and are instead dedicated to walkers, cyclists, horse riders and skaters.

A walk in the woods is unthinkable without a place to stop for refreshment. This was also already the motto by the end of the 19th century, and the first Chalet Robinson was built in 1877: a two-storey wooden house in the style of a Swiss chalet, on an island in a manmade lake in the middle of the woods. The original building was burned down in 1991. It was rebuilt, true to the original, in 2009, again as a restaurant with a big beer garden. And because it is on a small island, it can only be reached by one of two electric ferries.

The Chalet Robinson is a popular and peaceful spot, despite being close to the city centre, as the destination of a walk or to round off a lovely summer evening. You can eat and drink, sit in the sun and enjoy the view or rent one of the many boats and row around the island. The house may appear rustic from the outside, but inside it is modern and functional. Arriving guests are greeted by a double portrait of the young Jackie Kennedy to the right of the entrance and there is a ballroom and events hall on the upper floor.

Address Sentier de l'Embarcadère / Steigerweg 1, 1000 Brussels, +32 (0)2 3729292 | Getting there Tram 25 or 94, or bus 41 to Brésil | Hours Mon–Sat noon–11pm, Sun 11am–11pm | Tip The meadow to the north of the lake near the ice rink and Jeux d'Hiver is called La Pelouse des Anglais (The English Lawn). A bronze plate recollects a cricket match that English soldiers played here on 17 June, 1815, on the eve of the Battle of Waterloo.

20__Chez Vincent

Through the kitchen into Brel's favourite restaurant

The two wings of the Royal Galleries are separated by the Rue des Bouchers / Beenhouwersstraat. And 'Butcher Street' certainly does justice to its name, being, as it is, Brussels' restaurant hotspot. Here you will find one eatery after another, on both sides of the street, as well as in the side streets. There are famous restaurants such as the Aux Armes de Bruxelles, many, quite rightly, unknown places, but also good ones such as l'Ogenblik or Scheltema. Food is and remains a matter of taste after all.

Chez Vincent in Rue des Dominicains – a simple rotisserie, according to the lettering on the window – could definitely not be described accurately by the phrase 'a matter of taste'. There is nothing quite like it, as Jacques Brel attested. You enter the restaurant through the kitchen – there is no other way in – immediately finding yourself in the heart of the action. Hustle and bustle, chefs, waiters, lots of copper and brass, steam and bubbling – it soon becomes clear that cooking is a combination of art and hard work. Beyond the kitchen are two saloons – the smaller one is panelled with dark wood, intimate and also quiet, the larger one feels a bit like a brewery, but its appearance is unparalleled. It is tiled completely with faience, produced at the founding of the restaurant in 1905. The end wall presents the restaurant's emblem, a fishing boat in a storm, across 20 square metres; the left is adorned with a horseman on the beach of Ostend, combing mussels from the sand, and the right a Flemish landscape scene.

Whether mussels, fish or meat, flambéed at the table or roasted, the meals are of high quality, the prices – for Brussels' standards – not excessive and the service good. And in your head you will hear, spontaneously, the melody of Vlakke Land or Marieke, and you can almost see Brel drinking a glass of red wine or Orval at his regular table in the corner.

Address Rue des Dominicains / Dominikanenstraat 8–10, 1000 Brussels, +32 (0)2 5112607, www.restaurantvincent.be | Getting there Metro 3 or 5 to Gare Centrale / Centraal Station | Hours Daily, apart from Tue, noon–3pm & 6.30–11pm | Tip In contrast, Belga Queen at Rue du Fossé aux Loups / Wolvengracht 32, conveys pure luxury: a classy restaurant and an oyster bar in the sumptuously renovated former counter hall of the 18th-century Crédit du Nord bank.

21 __ The Chip Shop

Even the German Chancellor once stood in the queue

The name is a little misleading. Maison Antoine is definitely not a house, it is a chip shop, no, *the* chip shop in Brussels. An institution. It's a cast-iron guaranteed fact that Angela Merkel, just like every other customer, stood and waited patiently in the queue here to refuel with a bag of pommes frites during a break at an EU summit. Waiting in line in front of this pavilion is quite common, and it has been since 1948. A Baraque à Frites or Fritkot under the name Antoine has stood here on Place Jourdan since then. It's always been busy. And because the square is right in the middle of the European quarter, just beneath the Parliament and Commission buildings, overhearing some tittle-tattle between politicians waiting here in the queue isn't all that rare.

The fries come – as is good and proper – in a paper cone (cornet), because they soak up more fat than a polystyrene tray (ravier) and don't leave your hands covered in ink like the traditional newspaper. Of course, only fresh potatoes are used, and of course they are fried twice, in beef dripping: once to cook them, after which they are left to cool, before being thrown back into the oil for a second time to brown. If they were only fried once, they would either be under cooked or burnt. No Belgian would seriously consider either of those options as edible.

That is also the case for plain old salt and vinegar, or even ketchup and mayonnaise. Here you can get either sauce, or mustard if that's your thing, but they aren't really common in Belgium. Belgians prefer tartare sauce with chives or spicy sauces: Andalouse, Americaine, chilli, piri piri and samurai in ascending order. As a good Fritkot, Maison Antoine has around 50 different sauces on offer. As well as pommes frites and frikandel, they also serve meatballs, chicken skewers, shashlik, merguez, Ardennaise sausage and many other delicacies.

Address Place Jourdan 1, 1040 Brussels (Etterbeek), +32 (0)2 2305456 | **Getting there** Metro 1 or 5 to Schuman or bus 59, 60 or 80 to Jourdan | **Hours** Sun–Thu 11.30–1am, Fri & Sat 11.30–2am | **Tip** It is common to take your chips to one of the surrounding bars so you can enjoy them with their ideal partner, a cold beer. A list on the pavilion contains the bars that are certain to be accommodating.

22___Cité Hellemans

Social housing development in Bauhaus style

At the beginning of the 19th century, Belgium was a trailblazer in the first industrial revolution and had the second largest industry in Europe after England. Thousands of people moved into the cities in search of work. Brussels, still largely medieval, with its narrow, winding alleyways and no recognisable structure, was fit to burst at the seams. City centre slums formed, the grimmest of which was the Marollen. Those who lived here had nothing to lose. Neither the police nor fire brigade dared enter the neighbourhood. Parallel to the building of the Palace of Justice above the Marollen, the city council forged an axis, Rue Blaes, over a kilometre long and straight as a die, right through the middle of the neighbourhood, mainly to be able to better control the people here. However, it did nothing to change their plight.

The architect Emile Hellemans (1853 – 1926) planned a revolutionary project right here beginning in 1905: rather than displacing the poor from their neighbourhoods, the policy was to demolish the slums and construct new rental flats. On the initiative of the socialist movement one of the first social housing associations was created, and it constructed the Cité Hellemans between 1912 and 1915: seven parallel lines of red-brick houses with coloured decorative borders in the heart of the city. The rows were separated by streets exclusively for pedestrian use and connected to one another by archways. In total, 272 apartments were created, each equipped with running water, bathroom, their own balcony and cellar. This provided a revolutionary living standard, not only for the Marollen of the early 20th century. The complex was completely renovated in the middle of the 1990s.

Today, Cité Hellemans is a hidden gem, loved and coveted among its residents, right next to the daily flea market on Place du Jeu de Balle.

Address Rue Blaes / corner of Rue de la Rasière, 1000 Brussels | Getting there Metro 2 or 6 to Porte de Hal / Halleport or bus 27 or 48 to Hôpital Saint-Pierre (Rue Haute) or Jeu de Balle (Rue Blaes) | Hours Accessible 24 hours | Tip The parents of jazz icon Jean 'Toots' Thielemans run the pub 't Trapken af at Rue Haute / Hoogstraat 241. This is where 'little Toots' discovered his passion for jazz and the harmonica.

23__ The Cloister

A paradise for all the senses in Rouge-Cloître

The park Forêt de Soignes/Zoniënwoud, only 10 kilometres away from the centre of Brussels, is one of the most well-kept forests in Belgium with a lavish stock of trees. You will find the 14th-century Abbey of Rouge-Cloître, the red cloister, so called because it was built with red mortar, in the northern part of this green oasis. The Augustinian monks cultivated the surrounding land, created ponds and operated a prolific agricultural business, which also supplied nearby Brussels. The abbey has also always been a refuge of art, of writing and painting. The author Jean Gielemans (1427–1487) once lived here, a prestigious library is maintained, and one of the most famous painters of his time, Hugo van der Goes (1435–1482), who had joined the Order of Saint Augustine in 1476, painted numerous important paintings here.

The abbey existed until its dissolution by the French in 1796 and the church was completely destroyed in 1834 through pillaging and looting. The cloister has been home to a cotton mill, then a munitions factory, and finally a hotel and restaurant at the end of the 19th century. Today it presents itself, after being completely renovated in the 1990s, as a self-contained ensemble of buildings and gardens. The priory has been returned to the condition it was in at the end of the 18th century, when it was still inhabited by Augustinian monks. The cloister can be seen in the architecture of the late 17th century, the gatehouse and the building for the lay brothers in that of the 15th century. Rouge-Cloître went into state ownership in 1910 and today the City of Brussels uses it as a cultural centre.

Around a dozen artists, glass blowers and painters work here in cheap studios, the cloister's farmers also take care of the six-hectare park and a riding school is in operation. There are also regular exhibitions of modern art.

Address Centre d'Art de Rouge-Cloître, Rue du Rouge-Cloître / Rood-Kloosterstraat 4, 1160 Brussels (Auderghem / Oudergem), +32 (0)2 6605597, www.rouge-cloitre.be | Getting there Metro 5 to Hermann-Debroux, tram 44 or bus 74 or 72 to Auderghem-Foret | Hours Centre d'Art: Tue – Thu, Sat & Sun 2 – 5pm | Tip The forest, which covers over 4,000 hectares with its fabulous stock of trees, is wonderful for long walks.

24_ The Clothes Collection

When the Manneken Pis *gets dressed up*

There aren't many people in the world who have a wardrobe as large and diverse as the *Manneken Pis*. As a diplomatic present, on official or secret missions, on special national and international occasions or when faced with events in Brussels – the emblem of the city has been fitted with clothing of every imaginable kind for centuries. Whether in trousers, cloak, dress or uniform – the boy's little penis is always under his left hand, sticking out of the fly or through the gown, threatening to pee on the viewer at the drop of a hat.

You can view the extensive wardrobe of probably the most prominent citizen of Brussels in a dedicated room of the Musée de la Ville, the city museum, on the north side of the Grand-Place. Replicas behind glass are clothed in the most unbelievable outfits. *Manneken Pis* has been dressed up as an artist and a clown, as a Brit with a Union Jack and top hat, as a footballer, ice hockey player, Eskimo, maharajah and oriental prince, as a doctor, policeman and soldier, as a gaucho, cowboy and sultan, in prizewinning designer looks and as a member of the Belgian team for the 2016 Olympic Games in Rio de Janeiro. And there are endless cupboards and glass display cases full of the unusual garb that the little man has already worn. Around 800 costumes belong to the *Manneken Pis'* collection, which can also be admired interactively at multimedia terminals.

There are several legends concerning the little urinator atop the city-centre fountain, who has been re-clothed time and again since the early 17th century. A first inventory of his wardrobe goes back to the year 1756, when the *Manneken Pis* got dressed up at least four times a year.

To this day, the *Manneken Pis* may only be dressed by an employee of the city. They clearly stay pretty busy, as there are years in which his outfit changes up to two dozen times.

Address Musée de la Ville de Bruxelles, Maison du Roi, Grand-Place, 1000 Brussels, +32 (0)2 2794350, www.brusselscitymuseum.brussels/fr | Getting there Metro 3 or 4 to Bourse/Beurs or metro 1 or 5 to De Brouckère | Hours Tue–Sun 10am–5pm, Thu 10am–8pm | Tip It is worth taking a closer look at the building, which was built at the start of the 16th century under Charles V and reconstructed in a Neo-Gothic style in the 19th century.

25_ The Comic Wall
Offbeat art in public space

Are comics art or just trash? Such questions aren't really taken seriously in Belgium. Comics or bandes dessinées are quite obviously the 'ninth art'.

The Institut Saint-Luc art school has been offering numerous courses on illustration since the end of the 1960s; the first teachers were Hergé (1907–1983) and Eddy Paape (the creators of *Tintin and Luc Orient* respectively). Comic illustration has been an official subject since 1976. Brussels sees itself as the capital of the comic and this is something you can literally go out and see. Throughout the city centre there are over 50 so-called murals, house walls that are painted partially or completely with figures by famous Belgian illustrators. And there are always new ones popping up, authorised by the city and the artists.

The ultimate Brussels figure is Tintin, the young reporter and adventurer, who travels the world solving mysteries with his little dog Snowy. You will find Tintin, Snowy and Captain Haddock climbing down a fire escape in der Rue de l'Étuve in a scene from *The Calculus Affair*. Brussels is the reporter's home, so the city's streets, buildings or parks also appear time and again in the albums. Since 2007 Tintin has been riding on a train, in black and white, on a wall in Midi train station – a scene from the book *Tintin in America*. Another picture by Hergé – the phonetic spelling of the word you get from swapping the initials of his real name Georges Remi and reading them in French – *Saint Nicolas' Visit to Brussels*, adorns the walls of Luxembourg railway station.

Guided tours to the various murals of the world-famous characters invented in Brussels, from Lucky Luke to the Smurfs, are available by bike or on foot. There's even a mural of Asterix and Obelix. You can also walk in the footprints of Tintin and Snowy. And beware – an annual comic festival takes over the city every autumn.

Address Rue de l'Étuve/Stoofstraat 37, 1000 Brussels | Getting there Bus 48 or 95 to Parlement Bruxellois | Hours Accessible 24 hours | Tip The modern Musée Hergé, around 20 kilometres east of Brussels in the university city of Louvain-la-Neuve, is completely dedicated to the work of the illustrator.

26_ Comme Chez Soi

The place in the kitchen

There must be many family restaurants that can look back on a 90-year history; but those that have also been continually awarded with Michelin stars and Gault-Millau toques for over 60 years must be rather rare. For good measure, the guests at Comme chez Soi can eat in the kitchen. The name is the game here – it's just like at home.

The manager Laurence Rigolet welcomes her guests at the door and shows them to their tables. The rather small dining area to the right of the entrance is an attraction in its own right: pure Art Nouveau, from the back-lit glass mosaic ceiling to the wooden separators between the tables. It is even more exciting, however, if you go straight on into the kitchen, as you can also sit and eat here, with space for a good 20 people, on one of the wooden tables decked in white, right next to the stainless steel kitchen counter. It certainly enhances the enjoyment. A dozen cooks stir, roast, boil and arrange the dishes under the supervision of head chef Lionel Rigolet. It all happens astonishingly quietly, there are no loud instructions and you are more likely to hear a cream being whipped or a sauce frothed up. It all conveys the impression of a finely balanced machine, as one cog fits perfectly with another and one movement is complemented by the next. And then there's the very subtle smell of the dishes that will be presented to the guests a short time later. Watching this kitchen ballet is very pleasing, almost as much as the food itself.

The service in the kitchen is of the same quality as in the actual restaurant. It is attentive but not overly assertive. No question, a visit to such a restaurant is an expensive pleasure, especially as the wine menu is also quite extraordinary. Over 26,000 bottles are stored in the cellar, which can be viewed on request, including several very special treasures.

Address Place Rouppe 23, 1000 Brussels, +32 (0)2 5122921, www.commechezsoi.be |
Getting there Tram 3, 4 or 32, or bus 46 or 86 to Anneessens | **Hours** Tue – Sat 7 – 9pm,
also Thu – Sat noon – 1pm (first and last admission) | **Tip** Booze 'n' Blues is the name of the
tiny corner pub on Rue de la Grande Île / Groot- Eilandstraat, corner of Rue des Riches
Claires. The name says it all here too: shots and blues music.

27__The Concert Hall

Sounds from the underworld in Henry Le Bœuf

The concert hall Henry Le Bœuf was inaugurated on 19 October, 1929, and since then, anyone with a name in the world of classical music has played here, from Rachmaninov and Stravinsky to Menuhin and Barenboim, who gave a solo concert here at the age of just 14. The auditorium, with its 2,100 seats, is said to have outstanding acoustics, especially after its thorough renovation in 2000.

The concert hall is only one of several event spaces in the huge, 8,000-square-metre cultural palace Bozar. The name Bozar is the phonetic spelling of the French name (Palais des) Beaux Arts, Palace of Fine Arts. It was an attempt to address both French and Flemish-speaking Belgians. According to the audience's reception, it worked: the Bozar is the centre of Brussels' cultural life, especially the Henry Le Bœuf concert hall.

When Victor Horta built the Palais between 1920 and 1928, this success story couldn't have been predicted. On the contrary, there was considerable resistance to overcome: no plot, no interest and no public money. Ultimately, private patrons of the arts jumped in, above all the banker Henry Le Bœuf (1874–1935) from Schaerbeek. The city offered a hillside plot that was considered unsuitable for building, and the king insisted that any potential building should not impair the view from his city palace at the upper end of the slope. Stepping through the main entrance at the foot of the former slope today, there is no sign of the huge problems financing it or the difficulties of building on the plot. The house was literally dug into the hill. The large concert hall is therefore practically underground. Those who climb the flight of stairs up to the orchestra stalls don't notice that either.

But you may become slightly confused if your seat is in one of the boxes on the balcony, as you go two steps down from what feels like ground level.

Address Henry Le Bœuf in Bozar, Rue Ravenstein 23, 1000 Brussels, +32 (0)2 5078200, www.bozar.be | Getting there Metro 1 or 5 or tram 92, 93 or 94 to Gare Centrale/Centraal Station | Hours Tue–Sun 10am–6pm, Thu 10am–9pm | Tip Under the nearby Place Royale and today's palace you can view the Coudenberg, the foundations of the royal palace from the 12th century, burned down in 1731, with Charles V's Aula Magna.

28__The Couple
Candid and aesthetic in front of the Finance Tower

On a small plinth, which looks like a landing, two women, young and beautiful, naked and graceful, stand hugging each other self-confidently and devotedly, while one of them seems, almost arrogantly, to suggest to the viewer that they can keep their voyeuristic glances to themselves. It is therefore no surprise that the unveiling of this four-metre-tall and widely visible sculpture in front of the Finance Tower on Boulevard du Jardin Botanique in 1984 led to vehement annoyance and all kinds of protests. There is no question: the sculpture is spectacular and provocative in its aesthetic quality, but also in its impact and candour.

On the commission of the investors of the Finance Tower – which was built in its current form in 1983, completely renovated again in 2006 and is to this day the second tallest high-rise in Brussels, indeed the whole of Belgium – the sculptor Nat Neujean, born in Antwerp in 1923, designed the bronze sculpture *L'Ame Sentinelle* between 1982 and 1984 as a percent-for-art installation. It certainly does justice to the 18-storey building in terms of its size and presentation. Nat Neujean had made a name for himself internationally, in particular in the USA, with his spectacular sculptures, which are to be found in many large collections. *L'Ame Sentinelle*, the closely embracing female couple, was inspired by the 1872 poem 'L'Eternité' by the rebellious poet Arthur Rimbaud (1854–1891). Neujean wanted his work to be understood as a tribute to the author. *L'Ame Sentinelle* was cast in bronze by the renowned Milan foundry De Andreis.

There is more art by Nat Neujean to be found in Brussels, such as the sculptures *Tintin* and *Snowy* in the Brussels Comic Museum from 1954 or in Parc du Wolvendael in Uccle (1976) as well as the bust of the politician and great European Robert Schuman (1886–1963) in Jubelpark from 1987.

Address Boulevard du Jardin Botanique / Kruidtuinlaan 50, 1000 Brussels | Getting there Metro 2 or 6 to Botanique | Hours Accessible 24 hours | Tip The Brussels Toy Museum (Musée du Jouet) is housed in the nearby Rue de l'Association 24 and is open daily 10am–1pm & 2–6pm.

29 __ The Cultural Palace

Lively parties in a botanical glass pavilion

Le Botanique – or 'le Bota' for short – is a Brussels institution with an eventful history. The glass palace by architect Charles-Henri Petersen (1792–1859) was inaugurated in 1829 as the orangery of a new botanical garden after a three-year construction period. An initiative by well-to-do citizens had financed the site, the building and the installation of a park on the crossroads of Rue Royale and the city ring road and gifted it to the city. The author Victor Hugo described the glass palace as a new world wonder. During the day, flowers were grown in the glasshouse and sold in bulk – in the evenings the bourgeois elite threw huge balls and enjoyed concerts.

In 1870, the Belgian state took over the site, made it into the National Botanical Gardens and furnished it with natural scientist Carl Friedrich Philipp von Martius' herbarium, which was famous at the time. The glasshouses now served agricultural research. Its most well-known success was the cultivation of chicory – it is now hard to imagine Belgian cuisine without it. In 1958, the National Botanical Gardens was relocated, out of the city centre to the suburb of Meise, and the glass palace was no longer used. A difficult period began, which very nearly ended with this little treasure being pulled down. It wasn't until 1984 that Le Botanique reopened, now as a cultural centre.

Around 300 concerts take place here every year. The main hall in the orangery has space for around 700 people; the amphi-theatre-like Rotonde holds 250, and the Witloof Bar offers standing room for 200. Musicians such as Oasis, Prince and Lou Reed all appreciated the intimate atmosphere this provides. The festival season in Brussels opens every year in May with the 'nuits botaniques', 10 days with around 60 concerts. The house hosts Café Bota, a museum and a gallery, which is used in particular for photographic exhibitions.

Address Botanique, Rue Royale / Koningsstraat 236, 1210 Brussels (Saint-Josse / Sint-Joost), +32 (0)2 2183732, www.botanique.be | **Getting there** Metro 2 or 6, tram 92 or 93 or bus 61 to Botanique / Kruidtuin | **Hours** The gardens and Café Bota are open during the day, the halls according to respective events | **Tip** The Cirque Royale is another round concert hall (Rue de l'Enseignement / Onderrichtstraat 81).

30__The Death of Marat

Jacques–Louis David's spectacular success from 1793

The Death of Marat is one of the most outstanding testimonies to the turmoil surrounding the French Revolution. It depicts the dying Jean-Paul Marat (1743–1793), the radical revolutionary, Jacobin and from 1792 elected member of the French National Convention, naked in his bathtub on 13 July, 1793. He had, a few minutes previously, been stabbed with a kitchen knife by the 25-year-old aristocrat Charlotte de Corday, who had deviously gained access to Marat's apartment by means of a letter. Marat, who suffered from a chronic skin condition, often spent several hours a day in the bath, where he also wrote key revolutionary texts.

The historical painter Jacques-Louis David (1748–1825), a close friend of the revolutionary, began the painting just one day after his murder. David had visited Marat for the last time a day before his bloody end – in the bathroom. After almost three months, the classical-style oil painting (162 by 128 centimetres) was finished and was hung on the end wall of the National Convention above the President's chair. The picture depicts Marat in the dying pose of a martyr of the revolution, in his hand the letter of admission with the name of the murderer. Just four days after the bloody deed, the Revolutionary Tribunal sentenced the young royalist de Corday to death by guillotine.

After the overthrow of the revolutionary Robespierre, the painting, which was also disseminated thousandfold as an engraving and became an icon of the French Revolution, was removed from the national collection and outlawed. David painted over it and hid it in the meantime, in order to save it from destruction. Later French governments of the early 19th century refused to purchase the picture. Finally, a nephew of Jacques-Louis David bequeathed it to the Royal Museum in Brussels in 1893, where the painter had spent the last years of his life.

Address Musée Royaux des Beaux Arts de Belgique, Rue de la Régence/Regent-schapsstraat 3, 1000 Brussels | **Getting there** Metro 1 or 5 to Gare Centrale/Centraal Station and Parc/Park or Tram 92 or 94 to Royale | **Hours** Tue–Fri 10am–5pm, Sat & Sun 10am–6pm | **Tip** The Royal Museum of Fine Arts has many treasures and is worth an extensive visit. You certainly mustn't miss the works of Pieter Bruegel the Elder, Hieronymus Bosch and Hans Memling on the 'Old Masters' floor.

31 The Dinosaurs

Europe's biggest dinosaur parade

Lots and lots of high-end technology, the most modern forms of presentation with multimedia installations and interactive games, all packed into huge futuristic halls – and yet it is a look back deep into the past, at the history of the Earth and life itself. It is a vision of the Triassic, Jurassic and Cretaceous periods, the building blocks of prehistoric life, part real, part computer animated, that has a hint of Disneyworld about it. Particularly spectacular is the dinosaur gallery, which has covered an area of over 4,000 square metres with a new and magnificent show since an elaborate restoration in 2007. Over 30 complete skeletons and fragments of dinosaurs of all sizes are on display – this is the world of the Diplodocus, Tyrannosaurus rex and Olorotitan.

Outstanding in every respect are the giant skeletons of the five-metre-tall Iguanodons, presented in an oversized glass cube. It is as if the creatures, which are millions of years old and are thought to have weighed up to 4,000 kilogrammes each, are about to move towards you.

The institute owns nine of these nigh on eight-metre-long giant plant eaters from the early Cretaceous period, which were found in the coal mines of Bernissart in the south of Belgium in 1878. This find was a sensation at the time, as only isolated footprints had been found until then, in far off regions such as England and Spitsbergen. Giant whale skeletons, fossilised lizards and huge turtles join the dinosaur parade. There's also a journey through the development of humankind.

The dinosaurs are the most spectacular section of the Royal Belgian Institute of Natural Sciences, founded in 1905. With around 37 million exhibits, including three million fossils, of which only a small proportion can be shown, this is, after Paris and London, the third-biggest natural science collection in the world.

Address Museum of Natural Sciences, Rue Vautier 29, 1000 Brussels, +32 (0)2 6274211, www.naturalsciences.be | Getting there Metro 2 or 6 to Trône / Troon, metro 1 or 5 to Maelbeek / Maalbeek or bus 34 or 80 to Museum | Hours Tue–Fri 9.30am–5pm, Sat & Sun 10am–6pm | Tip You can also visit the big museum shop without paying admission.

32 — The Diving Pool
Deep down underwater in the middle of the city

Jules Verne served as the patron in the choice of name: the diving centre that opened in the district of Uccle-Stalle in 2004 is called Nemo 33. Until two years ago it housed the deepest indoor diving pool in the world. There is now an even deeper one in Italy. The tiled, freshwater pool is gigantic all the same: it contains 2.5 million litres of non-chlorinated water, is 35 metres deep and measures 12 by 15 metres on the surface. At depth, and with water temperatures of at least 30 degrees, it separates into different sections. Caves fork off from the main pool, in some of which you can also surface; there are various windows through which the divers can look out of the pool, while visitors wave back.

The diver John Beernaerts already had the idea of a diving pool when he was a young man in 1978. At the time the reality, not only in Belgium, was of cold lakes and rivers with limited visibility up to a few metres and complete darkness from a depth of 15 metres; diving accidents were an issue, as well as diving teachers who believed that only those who overcame their fear of such conditions could become good divers.

It wasn't until 20 years later that Beernaerts got to work actually realising his idea and designed a pool that combined the greatest possible degree of safety with the joy of diving in tropical water temperatures.

Nemo 33 opened on 1 May, 2004. There are courses for beginners and advanced level divers as well as dives in groups at various degrees of difficulty. The water is safe to drink and environmental protection is a priority. Apart from the compulsory diving computer, all of the equipment can be borrowed free of charge. Your own water bottle or diving suits are not allowed, however, and towels, bags and photographic equipment must stay in the changing rooms. Making a prior reservation for dives is advisable, especially at weekends.

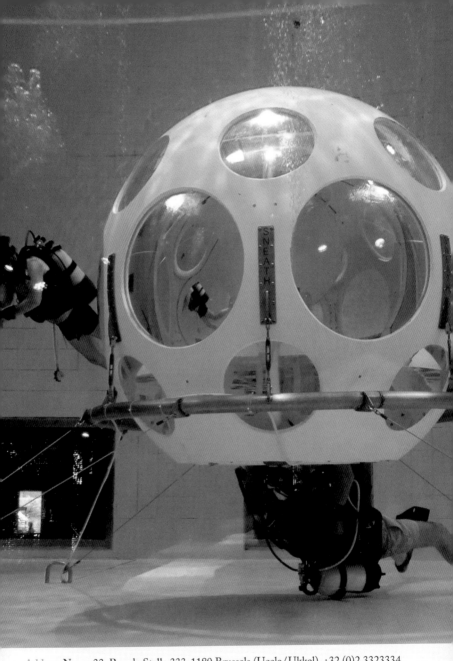

Address Nemo 33, Rue de Stalle 333, 1180 Brussels (Uccle/Ukkel), +32 (0)2 3323334, www.nemo33.com | Getting there Tram 4, 32, 82 or 97 or bus 98 to Carrefour Stalle | Hours Mon–Fr 10am–6pm, Sat & Sun 11am–6pm | Tip At YetiSki in Anderlecht you can polish your skiing and snowboarding technique in the middle of the city, come rain or shine, on a synthetic piste.

33__ The Dome
The Palace of Justice and the megalomania of Leopold II

On entering the gigantic entrance hall of Brussels' Palace of Justice, after first passing through the 40-metre-high portal and the security barriers that follow, you will suddenly feel very small. A huge space opens out, mighty flights of stairs lead to the upper floors, towering columns with austere capitals rise up to the 100-metre-high dome. How reassuring that in various corners and recesses of this monstrosity, lawyers and clients sit at long wooden tables, illuminated by the pale light of little green-shaded desk lamps – living people in this cosmos, which seems to engulf everything and is meant to put people in their place and always demands law abidance, merely through its brutal size.

This is what the power-hungry King Leopold II wanted when he awarded the architect Joseph Poelaert (1817–1879) the commission to realise this, the largest building in Brussels in the 19th century, for a lordly 50 million francs. The Palace of Justice was to be bigger than St Peter's Basilica in Rome – there are around 30 courtrooms, 250 rooms and numerous courtyards over 26,000 square metres.

The Palace of Justice, which was built between 1866 and 1883, is still fully operational to this day and still controversial. Not only because of the wild mix of different building styles, with classicalist and Baroque elements, and hints of Greek temple styles, Roman columns, emotional friezes and figures of historicism, of Baroque and Neo-Renaissance, but in particular because of the rigour of its construction. Around 3,000 houses in the district of Marollen, classically the neighbourhood of the workers and little people, were sacrificed for the Palace. The architect himself, a favourite of Leopold II, but reviled by locals as 'schieve architek' (crooked architect), died before the completion of this, his largest building, after apparently going insane.

Address Palais de Justice, Place Poelaert 1, 1000 Brussels | **Getting there** Metro 2 or 6 to Louise / Louiza or tram 92 or 94 to Place Poelaert | **Hours** Mon – Fri 8am – 5pm, closed in July | **Tip** You should also take a look at the 25-metre-high congress column on Place du Congrès, also built by Joseph Poelaert and five sculptors in 1850, which commemorates the constitutional convention of 1830.

34__ The Effigy of Mary
The Mother of God and the Ommegang

What is now one of the social highlights on the Brussels calendar, was originally a religious procession with a very special history. It has a close connection to Notre-Dame du Sablon church, a masterpiece of early Belgian Gothic architecture, and a woman whose name is all but forgotten nowadays in the frenzy of the Ommegang celebrations: Beatrijs Soetkens. According to the legend, Virgin Mary came to her in 1348 and called on her to steal a miracle-working Madonna from Antwerp and bring it to Brussels. The statue was to be erected in the small chapel of the crossbow guild, built in 1304 on a sand hill in front of the city gates in the Sablon quarter, as protection against the plague, which was spreading through Brabant. With the help of a sailor, the pious woman was able to bring the effigy of Mary to Brussels in a small boat via the Scheldt and the Senne. The effigy of Mary then became the patron saint of the crossbow guild, who pledged to conduct an annual procession, in which the statue is carried 'omme' (around) the church and into the city, in thanks. The miraculous Madonna attracted ever more believers – leading the rich crossbow guild to replace the chapel with a new, prestigious, richly furnished sacred building at the beginning of the 15th century: Notre-Dame du Sablon. Today the effigy – in the meantime a replica from the 17th century, the original having been destroyed by the iconoclastic Calvinists – can be viewed in the right portal of the church.

In 1549, the city authorities decided to organise a ceremonial procession of the aristocracy and the professions of Sablon to Grand-Place in honour of Emperor Charles V and his son Philip II, at the head, the crossbow men with the miraculous Madonna. The Ommegang, resurrected in 1930, in particular on the initiative of the high nobility, developed from this parade into its current form.

Address Notre-Dame du Sablon, Rue de la Régence/Regentschapsstraat 38, 1000 Brussels |
Getting there Metro 2 or 6 to Porte de Namur/Naamsepoort, tram 92 or 93 to Petit Sablon
or bus 27, 48 or 95 to Grand Sablon | Hours Daily 9am–6.30pm | Tip The 17th-century
tomb of the Thurn and Taxis family is well worth seeing. They held the monopoly of the
imperial postal service and made Brussels its centre, until it relocated to Regensburg in the
18th century.

35 The Empain Villa

The estate of the mega-rich bachelor

The mega-rich Empain family were known as 'the Belgian Rocke-fellers'. Baron Edouard Louis Empain (1852–1929) began as an engineer and made a fortune in railway construction. His company built and financed the Paris Metro, as well as tram systems in Lille, Cairo and Tashkent. The Empains operated mines in the Congo and Burundi and produced electricity around the world. In 1930, the illegitimate son of the baron, Louis Empain, 21 years old at the time and the richest bachelor in Belgium, commissioned the Belgian architect Michel Polak (1885–1948) to build the Villa Empain in the Embassy quarter just behind the Free University of Brussels. He created unimaginable luxury over 2,800 square metres of living space. On the outside: façades of polished Italian Baveno granite, gold-leafed edging, a horseshoe pool and a huge garden. Inside: pure marble, tropical and burl woods from India and Venezuela, glass mosaics and a back-lit glass ceiling by Max Ingrand (1908–1969). All of this is in the clear, strict lines of Art Deco.

The villa was ostentatious and overwhelming. This may be the reason that Louis Empain simply capitulated and took to his heels after receiving the keys to the villa in 1934. He emigrated to Canada and gifted the villa to the Belgian state only three years after its opening, with the condition that a museum be established in it. The architect Henry van de Velde was to carry out the repurposing. World War II thwarted these plans. The villa was first requisitioned by the German occupiers, converted to the home of the Russian embassy after the war, and finally into the headquarters and studio of the broadcaster RTL. In 2006, the Libyan-Armenian jeweller family Boghossian purchased the house for their foundation, renovated it elaborately, true to the original style, and created the current art and cultural centre for the promotion of East–West dialogue.

Address Avenue Franklin Roosevelt 67, 1000 Brussels, +32 (0)2 6275230, www.villaempain.com | Getting there Tram 25 or 94 to Marie-José or bus 71 to ULB | Hours Tue–Sun 11am–6pm | Tip Palais Stoclet (Avenue de Tervuren 281) is an imposing building. The architecture by the Viennese Josef Hoffmann and the interior design by Gustav Klimt are now protected on the UNESCO World Heritage List. The Palais is in private ownership and is not open to the public.

36__The Erasmus House

Dürer, Holbein and Bosch in a medieval homestead

Anderlecht, industrial city with 100,000 inhabitants, is now a district of Brussels, even though most locals would insist that they aren't from Brussels at all. In truth, Anderlecht is no more than five kilometres away from Grand-Place – in the Middle Ages, a one-hour walk from the city into the countryside.

In 1521 Erasmus of Rotterdam came here from the university city of Leuven in order to cure his continual fever, but also because he quite justifiably feared trouble for himself too after Martin Luther's excommunication.

When the great humanist sought refuge here for almost half a year, Anderlecht was a village with little more than 300 inhabitants. But as it was on St James' Way, the village grew quickly and even had its own beguinage, even if it was the smallest in the country. The Gothic brick house and yard in which Erasmus spent the summer of 1521, back directly onto this Beguinage. Both buildings together form one of the oldest museums in Belgium. It most recently received the visitors' award for museum of the year in 2009. On view is the oratory room, furnished in the style of the time, the Renaissance room, with paintings by Hieronymus Bosch and Pieter Huys, the study with famous Erasmus portraits by Dürer and Holbein and finally a library in the fresco room of the first floor with rare editions of works by the prolific Erasmus. The humanist critic of the church, pacifist and staunch European, wrote part of his *The Praise of Folly* here in Latin, as he most commonly did, rather than the more rarely used Greek.

The museum also has a medicine garden with over 100 medicinal plants from the time of Erasmus and a 'philosophical garden' with modern art, based on Erasmus' treatises. According to one 'you must be born a king or a fool', and another states 'I am a citizen of the world, known to all and to all a stranger'.

Address Rue du Chapitre / Kapittelstraat 31, 1070 Brussels (Anderlecht), +32 (0)2 5211383, www.erasmushouse.museum | Getting there Metro 5, tram 81 to Saint-Guidon / Sint-Guido or bus 49 to Maison d'Erasme | Hours Tue–Sun 10am–6pm; Beguinage 10am–noon & 2–5pm | Tip Espace Maurice Carême, named after the Walloon poet, is between the Erasmus House and the Beguinage and conducts scientific and cultural congresses. In the yard is a bust of the Cuban revolutionary José Martí.

37_The Evening Market

Drinking, eating and talking internationally on the Châtelain

Place du Châtelain is certainly neither one of the largest nor the most important, or even most attractive squares in the city. Yet here, in the neighbourhood of Ixelles, you will experience something quintessentially Brussels. The area behind the glamorous shopping street Avenue Louise has blossomed into one of the most popular residential areas in the city. There is lots of Art Nouveau architecture, including the beautiful three- and four-storey Belgian townhouses, Maisons de Maître. The streets are lined with good restaurants and pretty, modern shops – the area is loved by locals and newcomers alike.

The Wednesday market is Châtelain's big moment. The stalls are set up in the afternoon, selling fresh fruit, vegetables from the local area, all kinds of cheeses, olives, ham, sausage, oysters, flowers and wine – all in all a pretty farmers' market. But things only really start to get going from aperitif time, 6pm. People arrive straight from work and shopping becomes secondary. The neighbourhood comes together and people discuss their days, their lives, making the special charm of the city apparent in the process. Brussels is international, and many languages are spoken and broken here: French, Flemish, German, English, Greek, Spanish, Italian, all thrown together. When something isn't understood, people simply ask their neighbours for help translating. Groups meet up here, split up, and mix with other people. No one stays on their own. Most visitors to the market buy wine by the bottle and share it with their respective neighbours, whether they are friends or new faces. Some go after an hour, others stay. And talk. And eat. And drink. Until exactly 9pm, curfew for the market, which packs up without further ado. The fun continues in the surrounding pubs – many a shopping basket is forgotten and left sitting in one of the bars on the square after closing time.

Address Place du Châtelain/Kasteleinsplein, 1050 Brussels (Ixelles/Elsene) | Getting there Tram 81 or bus 54 to Trinité/Drievuldigheid or tram 93 or 94 to Bailli | Hours Wed from 5pm | Tip If you have time beforehand, don't miss Nijinski – a very special second-hand bookshop (Rue du Page/Edelknaapstraat 15).

38_ The Fabric Shop
The best cloth at the 'Green Dog'

There are people who only visit Brussels in order to shop in or seek inspiration from the 'Green Dog'. To be pedantic about it, we are in fact talking about two shops, Chien Vert and Chien du Chien, which are adjacent and connected to one another. Those who have shopped in these unusual fabric stores always come back for more.

Quai des Charbonnages, the coal quay, is in Molenbeek, right next to the Brussels–Charleroi canal in the old industrial quarter, formerly the home of the breweries and large warehouses. As industry shrank and production was relocated to the outskirts, the warehouses fell into disrepair. They were no longer needed. Molenbeek became poor and turned into an immigrant district, principally for people from northern Africa. Guy François discovered the charm of these halls in the 1990s. The son of a shipbuilder was selling fabric wholesale at the time. He rented a building without electricity or other similar luxuries right on the quay, at the crossroads of Rue du Chien Vert, for 'two-times nothing', in order to sell his fabrics to the public here too. Et voilà, a business idea and a brand name were born. The fabric from Chien Vert.

In the following years, François created a unique mixture of his passions for fabric, boats and architecture. Original sailing boats and fishing vessels hang from the ceiling of the shops, as a decorative measure and to set the scene for the fabrics. An East German Trabi, an aeroplane and a piano also serve this purpose, while cuts are made on old billiard and snooker tables. You can buy almost anything here, from real saris to fine lace or leather, fabrics for dresses or furniture upholstery, as well as buttons, ribbons and borders. But the best thing is: you don't have to love fabric or be able to tailor it to fall in love with these shops.

One hour in this colourful mix of style and beauty would make anyone happy.

Address Le Chien Vert, Rue du Chien Vert/Groene Hondstraat 2, 1080 Brussels (Molenbeek), +32 (0)2 4115439; Quai des Charbonnages 50a, 1080 Brussels, +32 (0)2 4148400, www.chienvert.com | Getting there Metro 1 or 5 to Comte de Flandre/Graaf van Vlaanderen or tram 51 to Petit Château | Hours Mon–Sat 10am–6pm | Tip Other businesses have also discovered the attraction of the old halls on the quay, such as Depot Design or Hotel Meininger in the former Bellevue brewery. The new Museum MIMA right out front is dedicated to the role of the Internet in modern culture.

39 __ The Fish Market

Lots of fish but little water

If you ask a local for the Quai aux Briques or the Quai au Bois à Brûler, you might just get a sheepish shrug of the shoulders in reply. Very few know the official name of the two former harbour quays flanking the square that everyone calls Fish Market or Sainte-Cathérine. Both names are misleading: Sainte-Cathérine is the name of the metro station, but Sainte-Cathérine square is to the right of the church entrance. And there hasn't been a fish market for more than 100 years. But this is where Brussels harbour lay in the Middle Ages. Later, the Brussels–Charleroi canal penetrated deep into the city at this point. Building materials such as stone (briques) and wood (bois à brûler) were dredged right up to the church walls, until the harbour basin was filled in.

The square is famous for its fish restaurants; there must be at least three-dozen all around it. There is something for every palate and wallet: whether it be lobster at François or Rugbyman, oysters in Les Crustacés or L'Huîtrière, hearty Belgian seafood cuisine at Bij den Boer or mussels and sea snails in Mer du Nord. In truth, everyone in Brussels has their own insider tip as to what tastes best where. There is consensus on one point though: be it fish soup, prawn croquettes or tomato crevette, the Fish Market whets the appetite and raises the spirits. The tendency is for prices to rise the closer you get to the church. But – as is the case in most places in Brussels – the lunch menu costs only a fraction of that stated on the dinner menu.

Since 1980, two water basins have been a reminder of the time when this was Brussels' harbour. From a bird's-eye view, you can still see that there is little more than 400 metres between them and the canal. All of the streets towards Yser / IJzer are called Quai / Kai and the big market halls remind you that this neighbourhood is the true heart of the city.

Address Marché aux Poissons/Vismarkt, 1000 Brussels | **Getting there** Metro 1/5 to Sainte-Cathérine/Sint-Katelijne | **Hours** Accessible 24 hours | **Tip** The annual Christmas market is very rewarding. Two old carousels, Manèges d'Andrea, make children and adults alike light up; a Ferris wheel offers the best view over the city, and there is also an ice-skating rink and lots of epicurean delights.

40_ The Flower Market

On Sundays, Brussels meets at Midi

If you go with the tourist flow through the streets and alleyways of Brussels, you will find the most astonishing shops. Practitioners of old-school crafts display their wares, from basket weavers and violin makers, to taxidermists. However, what you will rarely find, when compared with other European cities, are florists. Outsiders might even get the impression that the locals don't care much for plants.

But that's because very few tourists get to see the small, though lovingly cultivated gardens behind every Maison de Maître. The only other piece of evidence is the Sunday market at Gare du Midi. The market in the area around the train station, which is otherwise rather bleak, is one of the biggest in the city.

Fruit and vegetables are sold by the crate, as well as meat and sausage, cheese, fish and fowl – all the usual for a good weekly market. But most locals come here to buy plants. These can be found to the right of the railway bridge, under the colonnades. There are cut flowers of every colour and species, but especially potted plants for inside and out, bushes, shrubs and trees, from apple to quince, lemon to palm, box to rhododendron, as well as roses of course and seeds and seedlings for you to grow your own.

You'll often see people lugging six or more plastic bags full of plants, forcing their way through the crowds in the narrow passageways, trying to get to their cars as quickly as possible so that their freshly bought treasures don't start to wither before they reach the domestic garden.

'We Belgians are born with a brick in our bellies', according to a Brussels saying that refers to people's strong desire to buy or build their own house, no matter how small. And of course, there can be no house without a garden – and that needs looking after, even if the gardens of many townhouses cover an area little more than that of three towels.

Address Gare du Midi / Zuidstation, Esplanade d'Europe, 1000 Brussels | **Getting there** Metro 2 or 6, tram 3, 4, 32, 51, 81 or 82, or bus 27, 49, 50 or 78 to Gare du Midi / Zuidstation | **Hours** Sun 6am – 1pm | **Tip** Every second summer (in even years) a carpet of flowers made of hundreds of thousands of begonias is created on Grand-Place. Always on a weekend in August, always a new work of art. Best viewed from the balconies of the town hall and the Maison du Roi.

41__ The Foundry

Industrial culture in Molenbeek

In the 19th century, little Belgium was the leading industrial nation on the European continent. Only England was more highly developed. Walloon had coal and iron, Flanders harbours and trade links, and the capital Brussels was in fact an industrial metropolis. As early as 1835, the first European railway line linked the city with Mechelen. There were hundreds of factories along the canal. At the time the name Molenbeek didn't have connotations with Islamic terror, but rather with 'little Manchester', as the district is known locally.

The Foundry, an industrial museum in the renovated halls of a former bronze foundry, pays homage to this history. It is clear from the museum and the permanent exhibition that they have been thought out and developed by people who know the physical work involved well. Nothing is static or too theoretical. Visitors can and should touch the exhibits. For example, an old lathe, on which the brakes for the first cars, but later also for the airline company Lockheed in the USA, were manufactured. And then you find out that this lathe was used by Louise Windelinckx, a granddaughter of the company's founder, in order to create faithful reproduction brakes for vintage cars until 1994. The practical work with metal, wood or textiles is a part of the exhibition. Other themes are the organisation of the working world, the influence of industrial work on urban development and demography, and the role of gender. All in all, it is history to touch.

The museum has constantly grown over the past 30 years. In the yard, there are piles of old tools and machine parts that are being refurbished for new exhibitions. For 10 years an annual workshop has taught the artistic side of the craft under the title 'The History of Metal and Fire': at the appointed place metal becomes art, whether forged, formed or moulded.

Address La Fonderie, Rue Ransfort 27, 1080 Brussels (Molenbeek), +32 (0)2 4109950, www.lafonderie.be | Getting there Metro 1 or 5 to Comte de Flandre / Graaf van Vlaanderen, tram 51 to Port de Flandre or tram 82 or bus 86 to Triangle | Hours Tue – Fri 10am – 5pm, Sat & Sun 2 – 5pm | Tip La Fonderie also offers two-hour harbour tours – on a boat that used to sail on Lake Zürich – which enable a very special view of Brussels' industrial history.

42 ___ The Fountain of the Blind

An homage to Pieter Bruegel the Elder

The old-town alley Rue au Beurre/Boterstraat begins right behind the Bourse with the small church of Saint Nicolas. Picturesque and very medieval, it is completely surrounded with tiny houses and shops, which appear to be pushing up against the church walls.

On the corner in front of the baroque façade of the de Goude Huyve House is a fountain, one of the few in the city with drinking water. On top of the fountain is a sculpture by Jos de Decker (1912–2000) from Dendermonde, called *Les Aveugles* (The Blind). The three men, who seem to be feeling their way along, holding onto a stick with their faces turned up towards the sky, are not very big. They are, however, an unusual homage to one of the city's great painters, Pieter Bruegel the Elder (around 1525–1569), and his painting *The Blind Leading the Blind*. In turn, Bruegel's picture is citing the Gospel of Matthew in the Bible: 'If a blind man leads a blind man, both will fall into a pit'. If you want to see the original painting, you will have to travel a long way, to Naples to be precise, where it hangs on the walls of the Museo di Capodimonte. But this beautiful little fountain can be found right here in the centre of Brussels. And there are 10 homages to Bruegel like this all around the city. Those in the know stroll from one fountain to the next, trying to decipher the citations.

Two of them can be found only a few steps away on Place de Brouckère: *The Swing* (Jos de Decker) and *Leapfrog* (Jean Roig), both quotes from the Bruegel painting *Children's Games*. Then there is *The Fat Kitchen* on Nouveau Marché aux Grains and *Carnival* on Rue Rollebeek, *Dance* on Place du Jardin aux Fleurs and *Bagpipe Player* on Rue du Grand Hospice. There is a *Monkey* on Rue Haute and the *Harvest* on Marché aux Fromages/Kaasmarkt, *Gallantry* on Vieux Marché aux Grain/Oude Graanmarkt and the *Gossipers* on Rue des Renards/Vossenstraat.

Address Rue au Beurre/Boterstraat, 1000 Brussels | **Getting there** Metro 3 or 4 to Bourse/ Beurs | **Hours** Accessible 24 hours | **Tip** If you want more Bruegel, try the Royal Museum of Fine Arts or swing by the Bruegel family home at Rue Haute/Hoogstraat 132.

43_ Galerie Bortier

Fancy things for art lovers

Jean-Pierre Cluysenaar (1811–1880) is well known among specialists, but not necessarily world famous. The Dutch architect certainly made a name from himself in Brussels as an urban planner and renewer with two arcades, in particular the famous Galeries Saint-Hubert, but also with the much less well-known Galerie Bortier. It was originally, after its inauguration in 1848, part of a large shopping arcade between Kunstberg and Grand-Place, the Marchés Madeleine. In 1958, the majority of this arcade was developed into the City of Brussels ballroom and then converted into a modern concert hall in 2016. Today Galerie Bortier makes a small, covered arc from Rue Madeleine 55 to Rue Saint-Jean 19.

The first thing you will notice inside is the smell of old paper. There are no swanky shops or high-class boutiques in Galerie Bortier – all of the shops here trade in paper products. A paradise for lovers of old printed work. From folios or reference works from the pre-digital era, first editions or misprints, to classics or comics (the 'ninth art' is a cultural asset in Belgium) – you will find pretty much everything imaginable that can be printed on paper, mainly in French or Flemish of course, but occasionally also in English and other languages. You just have to do some digging. But that is what makes Galerie Bortier so special: visitors are welcome to rummage, touch, leaf through the offerings – in fact, they are even expressly expected to do so. And, of course, there is specialist advice and sales negotiations should it be needed.

This is also the case for the shops in the arcade that trade in prints and engravings. Some of the well-established antiquarian bookshops have recently found it hard to restock. Brussels does continue to be a real treasure trove for antiquities of all kinds, but the prices have, in places, risen more quickly than the income of potential buyers.

Address Rue de la Madeleine / Magdalenastraat 55, 1000 Brussels | **Getting there** Metro 1 or 5 or bus 29, 38, 63, 65, 66 or 71 to Gare Centrale / Centraal Station | **Hours** Daily 9am–6pm | **Tip** Passa Porta, at Rue Dansaert 46, is an international bookshop, which has put on an annual literature festival since 2004.

44__ The Glass Palace
The Royal glasshouses in Laeken

For a good three weeks a year, us 'mere mortals' have access to part of the Belgian royal family's private palace in Laeken: the glasshouses. Generally speaking, it is in April, just when the greatest amount of blossom can be expected – a great pleasure for all the senses.

The staked off and predefined path will lead you for more than one kilometre through 15 connected halls of steel and glass, filled with over 60,000 plants: palms, rubber trees and orchids, azaleas, but also indigenous flowers. It covers an impressive 15,000 square metres – that's the area of almost three football pitches. The large, free-standing dome of the so-called 'iron church' (also called the Winter Garden) in the centre of the complex stands on 36 columns and is 25 metres high.

The only glasshouses in the world that are bigger than these are the 'Gardens by the Bay' created 100 years later in Singapore. The temperature also leaves a lasting impression. Tropical plants need warmth and moisture, and visitors experience this too under the glass domes. Every year almost one million litres of oil is burned to keep them heated.

The halls themselves are also impressive: intricate steel-and-glass architecture, built between 1874 and 1895 by the court architect Alphonse Balat (1818–1895), with the assistance of the young Victor Horta, based on the model of the Crystal Palace in London. The Laeken glass palace is, however, twice as big. Its curved, organic forms, which constantly enable new insights and perspectives, are particularly captivating. But more still, the steel-glass construction is seen as the initial spark for Art Nouveau and also as an archetype for all later halls that are designed to create and protect climate zones. It is also true, however, that the beautiful glass palace was financed with blood money – Leopold II's profits from his brutal slave-based economy in the Congo.

Address Avenue du Parc Royal, 1020 Brussels (Laeken/Laken) | Getting there Tram 3 or 7 to Araucaria or bus 19, 55 or 230 to Serres Royales | Hours Daily 9.30am–3.30pm, Fri–Sun also 8–9.30pm; exact dates at www.belgien-tourismus.de | Tip The Japanese tower and the neighbouring Chinese pavilion, also in Laeken, are certainly worth a visit (Avenue Jules van Praet 44).

45__The Hall Of Mirrors
Jan Fabre's jewel-scarab beetles

It seems crazy and out of time, but is at the same time one of the most unusual objects of art in Brussels – and this in the Royal Palace of all places, or more precisely, in the historic Hall of Mirrors. In 2000, the Belgian artist and theatre director Jan Fabre, born in Antwerp in 1958, received the unusual commission, from Queen Paola herself, to furnish the large Hall of Mirrors with contemporary art and install a permanent piece of work.

The artist and the queen agreed on a complete redesign of the ceiling of the Hall of Mirrors, which had been white inside its stucco framing since 1909. And as Jan Fabre, known for spectacular performances and avant-garde dance, theatre and opera productions, didn't wish to simply create something arbitrary, he grasped the opportunity to bemuse, but ultimately delight the royal family and art critics alike. Always drawn to the symbolism of nature, he turned to the scarab, the beetle that the Ancient Egyptians considered godlike, with their intense iridescent green wing cases, which have repeatedly featured in Fabre's painting and illustrative work for years.

The beetles were first transported to Brussels and carefully prepared. The ceiling of the Hall of Mirrors was then covered, mosaic-like, with over a million tiny scarab wing cases, densely packed, in layers, shimmering in green, but also, depending on the incidence of light, blue and turquoise, yet always shiny. The huge crystal chandeliers hanging from the ceiling were also seamlessly decorated with scarab beetles. Over 30 assistants worked three months long on the beetle mosaic, after a two-year preparation phase, in which the dead insects were meticulously dissected and prepared. The ceremonial handover of the work of art took place in 2002, in what has served the Belgian royals as their Neo-Classical residence since 1830.

Address Palais Royal, Place de Palais/Paleizenplein, Rue Bréderode 16, 1000 Brussels, +32 (0)2 5512020 | Getting there Metro 1 or 5 to Gare Centrale/Centraal Station or metro 2 to Trône/Troon | Hours Only in the summer months, Tue–Sun 10.30am–4.30pm | Tip It's worth taking a proper look around the rest of the Royal Palace with its impressive collection of paintings from the 18th and 19th century, the extravagant parlours, the large gallery and the throne room.

46__ The Hammam
Moroccan steam room in Rue Gallait

A wellness area with an affiliated spa is part of the service range you would expect of a good hotel in Brussels, or anywhere else for that matter. However, those who wish to experience the pleasures of an original oriental hammam go to Le Riad in Schaerbeek.

Riad is the name of the traditional houses, built around courtyards, in the old-town of Marrakesh near to the famous Jemaa el-Fnaa market. Today they are often guest houses with their own steam rooms. And that is why Zehour Kharbouch, who comes from Morocco, called her hammam, which she founded in 2005, Le Riad. The house in Schaerbeek belonged to her family. A law firm moved out, and the lower floor stood empty. Without further ado, Zehour, who was almost 50 years old at the time, founded her own business, together with her son Movenis Boucham in the middle of Brussels – a Moroccan steam room with everything that entails: fragrances and aromas from fresh or dried herbs, massages with lather, peelings with black soap of olive and clay mud packs, all pure natural products, imported directly from Morocco. Of course, there is also a lounge area with hot mint tea and freshly pressed orange juice too. And naturally the hammam has different opening times for women and men.

Originally a hammam was the washing facility for a whole district; today it is a moment of personal luxury with body and skin care treatments. What has remained is the tradition of visiting the hammam in a group, to relax in the hot steam while chatting and laughing with one another. Contemplative silence is rather rare in Le Riad, but that is precisely what gives it the authentic feel of a real oriental hammam. Alongside the various types of massage, manicures and pedicures, hair epilation and hair dressing are also part of the service. French and Flemish is spoken, as well as English and some German.

Address Rue Gallait 29, 1030 Brussels (Schaerbeek), +32 (0)2 2480210, www.leriad.eu | **Getting there** Tram 25, 32, 55 or 62 or bus 93 to Liedts | **Hours** Women: Tue, Thu, Fri & Sun 10am–5pm; Wed & Sat 10am–11pm; Men: Tue, Thu, Fri & Sun 6–11pm; Mon 2–11pm | **Tip** Lovina Spa is a modern wellness centre in the Tour & Taxis halls with a sauna, steam room, massages and sunbeds.

47__Hell

Commemorating the Heysel Stadium disaster of 1985

It was 29 May, 1985, around two hours before kickoff in the European Cup Final between Liverpool and Juventus in Brussels' Heysel Stadium. The mood was heated. Tickets for Block Z, which was directly next to the section where Liverpool fans were seated and was actually supposed to be reserved for neutral spectators, were also sold, illegally, to Italians. Stones were thrown, flares and insults from both sides fired up the already aggressive atmosphere. Then, at around 7.45pm, hundreds of Liverpool fans charged at the Italians in Block Z. Within a few seconds the English hooligans tore down the inadequate wire-mesh fencing and chased after the Juventus fans. Mass panic broke out, people fell to the ground, were knocked over and trampled. The situation got out of control and the police were helpless. The fleeing Juventus fans searched for a way out and were pushed against a dilapidated concrete wall, which suddenly collapsed, burying many people under it. And all of this beamed out live to millions of people watching on television. The bloody outcome: 39 dead, 32 of them Italians, over 450 injured, some of them seriously. 'Heysel' became a synonym for the worst ever tragedy in European football.

The Heysel Stadium, which had opened in 1930, was largely closed down and ultimately torn down but for the façade, only reopening in 1995 under the name King Baudouin Stadium as a multifunctional arena with all the appropriate safety standards. A memorial plaque at the back of the stand commemorates those killed in the 1985 stadium disaster. In 2005, the French light designer Patrick Rimoux installed a 60-square-metre sundial sculpture in front of the stadium. Through the use of Italian and Belgian materials and an English poem as well as the names of the 39 people killed, the intention is to give expression to the grief of the three countries: 'Never forget'.

Address King Baudouin Stadium, Avenue de Marathon 135, 1020 Brussels (Heysel/ Heizel) | Getting there Metro 6 or 7 to Heysel/Heizel | Hours Viewable from the outside only | Tip There are two attractions between the stadium and Atomium: the Planetarium (Avenue de Bouchout/Boechoutlaan 10) and Mini-Europe (Bruparck).

48_ The Herb Shop

Where pharmacists and top chefs shop

The history of the herbalists Desmecht began in the old Flemish neighbourhood in 1840. The Desmecht family traded in various types of flour and meal, including phosphatine, the first baby food in powder form, right next to the Fish Market and Sint-Katelijnekerk. The townhouse's proud gable end heralds this history. Today the Desmecht family runs two health food shops in the city centre, one of them still in the original store.

The medicinal plant dealer's special service only becomes apparent in the back room of the original shop. Just like in an old pharmacy, the wall is completely made up of wooden drawers, 500 boxes in total. They are filled with herbs from all around the world, in dried or ground form, crushed or in whole pieces.

Hugo Desmecht mixes teas, medications and spices here, creating little clusters of aroma. His customers include specialist physicians who need specific ointments; Lionel Rigolet, the two-starred master chef at Comme Chez Soi, who is always on the lookout for special flavours for his creations; and the most varied of customers from all around the neighbourhood and the whole city. Each of them orders their own very personal mixtures for their individual demands.

Products range from special muesli (hard to find in Belgium) to pure honeys and organic cosmetics. The list of herbs is almost endless, from absinthe to zedoary, from well-known herbs such as rosemary and jasmine to broadly unknown ones such as ashwagandha.

Hugo Desmecht completed his alternative practitioner diploma at a state examination in the south of Germany – coincidently he was one of the first Belgians to do so. His daughter Ellen and son-in-law Niels also have the corresponding certificates. We can therefore happily assume that this mixture of traditional craft and modern knowledge will continue to be cultivated at Desmecht.

Address Herboristerie Desmecht, Place Sainte-Cathérine/Sint-Katelijneplein 10, 1000 Brussels, +32 (0)2 5112959, www.desmecht.com | Getting there Metro 1 or 5 to Sainte-Cathérine/Sint-Katelijne or metro 3 or 4 to Bourse/Beurs | Hours Tue – Sat 9.30am – 6pm | Tip The fish shop Mer du Nord/Noordzee is diagonally opposite. Here you have to eat on the street, but they do have the best mussels and oysters in the city – and will serve you a glass of cold white wine or Champagne on request.

49__The Hero

Being proud of the martyr Everard't Serclaes

If you touch the hero, your wish will be granted. But you mustn't ever say it out loud. Keep it to yourself and your wish will come true, or at least that's how legend would have it. No wonder that the figure of Everard 't Serclaes (circa 1320–1388), lord of Cruyckembourg, on the wall of a small passage just to the left of the Town Hall on the Grand-Place, exhibits several worn areas, particularly on his head and arms.

The monument, created in 1902, alongside the gravestone of copper and zinc, by the sculptor Julien Dillens (1849–1904), who was born in Antwerp and worked all his life in Saint-Gilles, shows the hero lying on his deathbed. He was ambushed and fatally wounded by his adversary Sweder d'Abcoude, the lord of Gaasbeek, and died on 31 March, 1388 in the adjoining Maison de l'Etoile, the 'House of the Star'. It wasn't long before he became a legend.

Everard 't Serclaes became revered as a hero during his lifetime. On 24 October, 1356 he captured the city walls with a small troop of likeminded citizens and freed Brussels from the interim Flemish rule of Count Louis de Male (1330–1384). He in turn had seized Brussels in the turmoil of the Brabant war of succession and installed himself in place of the next in line, Duchess Joanna. Duchess Joanna reciprocated her reinstatement, thanking the citizens of Brussels with the enactment of the 'Charte de la Joyeuse Entrée' (Charter of Joyous Entry), which enshrined civil rights and the duties of rulers, separated neatly and tidily from each other, in the country's laws for hundreds of years to follow.

Everard 't Serclaes, who was himself elected five times to juror of Brussels' town hall as reward for the liberation of the city, became a martyr and is venerated to this day. The scene of his murder is depicted once again in the courtyard of the town hall on the left door of the Leuven stairs.

Address Grand-Place, corner of Rue Charles Buls, 1000 Brussels | Getting there Metro 3 or 4 to Bourse/Beurs or metro 1 or 5 to Gare Centrale/Centraal Station | Hours Accessible 24 hours | Tip Next to the hero is a large commemorative plaque for the Brussels mayor Charles Buls (in office from 1881 to 1899), who was responsible for the magnificent restoration of the buildings on Grand-Place and is revered today as its 'saviour'.

50__ The Horsemen
Don Quixote and Sancho Panza

On a rather inconspicuous square, surrounded by numerous new hotel buildings between Gare Centrale and Grand-Place, the wanderer encounters two mounted journeymen. One of them on a horse, the other on a mule: Don Quixote and Sancho Panza. The two legendary figures from medieval Spanish literature trot through Brussels up high on top of a massive concrete pedestal next to the Spanish steps. The tall, haggard Don Quixote on his mare Rocinante and his groom Sancho Panza, united in the gallant battle 'against windmills' and ever new fictitious enemies. 'The knight with the sad countenance' was, in 1605, the great literary success of the Spanish national poet Miguel de Cervantes (1547–1616), a masterful parody of knightly ideals and the social structures of his time. In 1930, the Spanish sculptor Lorenzo Coullaut Valera (1876–1932) on the behest of King Alfonso XIII created a massive bronze statue of the two fantastic swashbucklers in front of the Cervantes Monument on the Plaza de España in Madrid.

But how did the two riders ever come to be in the Belgian capital? On the occasion of the Spanish presidency of the Council of the European Union in 1989, Spain presented the City of Brussels with an exact replica of the powerful bronze statue. It was intended as a reference to centuries of close association between Spanish Habsburg and Flemish Belgium, which was long part of the Spanish kingdom under the name 'Southern Netherlands'.

There is a second statue on the square, standing somewhat in the shadow of the two riders. It represents the Hungarian composer and antifascist Béla Bartok (1881–1945), and was moulded by the Hungarian sculptor Imre Varga, born in 1923. The sculpture was a gift from the City of Budapest on the occasion of the 50th anniversary of the composer's death in 1995. He had regularly spent time and written music in Brussels.

Address Place d'Espagne / Spanjeplein, 1000 Brussels | Getting there Metro 2 or 6 to Gare Centrale / Centraal Station | Hours Accessible 24 hours | Tip A quick look inside the nearby 13th-century Eglise Sainte Marie-Madeleine is definitely worthwhile (Rue de la Madeleine / Magdalenastratt).

51 The Horta Studio

The home of the Art Nouveau architect

The architect Victor Horta built his own private house at 23–25 Rue Americaine in the Brussels neighbourhood of Saint-Gilles between 1898 and 1901. It's a real gem in every sense. Unadulterated Art Nouveau, especially inside: every piece of furniture, every hinge, door handle, lamp, mosaic, glasswork and wall decoration precisely composed as a complete work of art, entirely consistent with Art Nouveau's concept of art and life. A stairwell doesn't simply bring light into the house, it veritably illuminates it.

Here you can see and experience first hand what the artists of the Vienna Secession, of the Weimar Bauhaus and of the Brussels Art Nouveau were trying to achieve. And that has not always been appreciated. In the 1960s, hundreds of Art Nouveau buildings were torn down in Brussels alone in order to make room for high-rise buildings. Almost none of the buildings by Henry van de Velde and Paul Hankar have been preserved, and even Victor Horta's world-famous Volkshaus / Maison du Peuple had to make way for an insurance company building despite fierce protests.

But fortunately the fate of his own home was different. The value placed on its design and thereby also on the craftsmanship of the carpenters, stonemasons and window builders is evident in every detail of the building and its furnishings. It was only the well-to-do middle class who could afford this kind of 'art house'. At the same time, the architect's political aim was to liberate working people from the darkness of the back yards. That is why the design of light plays a central role in Horta's work, and why he designed the biggest Art Nouveau building in Brussels, the Belgian Labour Party's 'House of the People'. A model in the Horta Museum is all that is left to remind us. At least three more Horta structures in Brussels, alongside his studio, are now protected on the UNESCO World Heritage List.

Address Horta Museum, Rue Américaine / Amerikaansestraat 25, 1060 Brussels (Saint-Gilles / Saint-Gillis), +32 (0)2 5430490, www.hortamuseum.be | **Getting there** Tram 81, 91, 92 or 97 or bus 54 to Place Janson | **Hours** Tue–Sun 2–5.30pm | **Tip** The best impression of Victor Horta's design of public buildings is conveyed by the former department store Waucquez in Rue des Sables / Zandstraat 20, today home to the comic museum Centre Belge de la Bande Dessinée.

52__Hôtel Tassel

Cornerstone of the European Art Nouveau metropolis

In 1893 Victor Horta designed Hôtel Tassel as a private house for the scientist Emile Tassel and became world famous almost overnight at only 32 years old. From the outside, the house doesn't look much different from neighbouring buildings, only the sweeping lines in stone and the profusion of glass stand out. But inside there isn't the slightest hint of 'narrow Brussels townhouse'. Instead, the stairwell is an exposed, organically curved cast-iron structure with a glass roof, which illuminates the whole house, making it feel spacious and elegant – a huge success in the effect and design of space by the man who was seen as the master of Belgian Art Nouveau from this point on. The innovative conceptualisation of his buildings as complete works of art caused a real stir. Every piece of furniture, even every door handle, became part of the architecture. Horta described the design as highly practical and in no way artistically affected.

Victor Horta (1861–1947) was born the son of a cobbler in Ghent. He received his first architecture prize, aged only 23, for the design of a Belgian parliament building that was never built. Many other awards followed. It was during his work on the concept of the Royal Greenhouses in Laeken as an assistant to architect Alphonse Balat that his skill in working with glass and steel first became clear. Initially he focused on public buildings, not wanting to build private houses for the rich. But everything changed with Hôtel Tassel, considered the first Art Nouveau building in the world. A phase of exemplary buildings followed, not only by Victor Horta, but also his friends Paul Hankar and Albert Roosenboom. Almost 100 buildings were built in the neighbouring districts of Saint-Gilles and Ixelles and more than three dozen of the best known are within walking distance of the Hôtel Tassel, between Rue Louisa and Place Brugmann.

Address Hôtel Tassel, Rue Paul-Emile-Janson 6, 1050 Brussels (Ixelles / Elsene) | **Getting there** Tram 93 or 94 to Defacqz | **Hours** Private property, so viewable from the outside only | **Tip** The tourist office offers a map with Art Nouveau tours for 5 euros. ARAU offers guided tours for 20 euros per person on Saturdays from 10am – 3pm, including interior viewings (+32 (0)2 2193345).

53__The House of European History

EU self-representation in a time of crisis

Brussels, which is certainly not lean in terms of museums, welcomed a new addition in 2017: the House of European History. There have been discussions since the middle of the 1990s as to how to do it, especially about where to begin with the representation of Europe's complex history without getting lost in endless and thus increasing irrelevance. Then in 2011 the ambitious project could actually begin: it was decided that the museum should concentrate on the 20th century and, after dictatorships, wars, attempts at democracy and fascism, emphasise the history of European integration, which is, despite all of the current upheavals, a magnificent success story. Alongside the representation of 20th-century history, there were to be sporadic excursions, to antique Rome for example, or to France during the Renaissance and the Enlightenment. The museum is dominated by the 4,000-square-metre permanent exhibition on the collective history of Europe in the 24 official languages of the European Union, but there are also changing exhibitions, guided tours and events.

The basis of the new museum complex is the Eastman building in Parc Léopold, named after George Eastman, the inventor of the Kodak camera. Benefactors and patrons had the Belgian architect Michel Polak (1885–1948) construct a grand building in Art Deco style for a dental clinic here in 1935, which was to provide free dental care to the poor and disadvantaged children of Brussels.

The concept by the Paris architecture studio Chaix & Morel, in a planning consortium with Cologne-based JSWD Architekten, was based on the expansion of the Eastman building. At the centre is a transparent museum cuboid with a shimmering glass shell and container-like boxes that appear to be levitating. They create a fascinating asymmetric effect inside the uniform cuboid.

Address House of European History, Rue Belliard / Belliardstraat 135, 1000 Brussels |
Getting there Metro 1 or 5 to Maelbeek and Schuman, metro 2 or 6 to Trône / Troon
or bus 22, 27, 34, 38, 6 or 80 to European Parliament | Hours Mon 1–6pm, Tue–Fri
9am–6pm, Sat & Sun 10am–6pm, admission free | Tip Particularly appealing are the
carefully restored wall paintings by the artist Camille Barthélemy (1890–1961) of fables
by the medieval French author Jean de La Fontaine in the old waiting room of the former
Eastman dental clinic.

54 __ The Knight

Godfrey of Bouillon fighting a losing battle

Godfrey of Bouillon is actually a central figure in Brussels public life, and his equestrian statue couldn't possibly be more present than here on the historic Place Royale above the Mont des Arts, not far from the Royal Palace. And yet the knight leads an isolated, lonely life, or in other words: the locals hardly take any notice of him, even though cars, buses and trams perpetually rush past him. There he sits, the Duke of Lower Lorraine, leader of the First Crusade of 1097, conqueror and first ruler of the Kingdom of Jerusalem, proud and self-confident in the middle of the square against the backdrop of the six Corinthian columns of the court church Saint-Jacques-sur-Coudenberg, which was consecrated in 1787, and he is practically ignored, except for the fact that he obstructs the traffic. The mighty equestrian statue was built in 1848 by Belgian sculptor Eugène Simonis (1810–1872), who also designed the lions on the foot of the congress columns and the gable of the Théâtre La Monnaie.

The Place Royale was completely redesigned in a Neo-Classical style by the French architect Gilles-Barnabé Guimard (1739–1805), beginning in 1774, on behalf of the Austrian general governor at the time Prince Charles Alexander of Lorraine. It was built on the foundations of the old Coudenberg Palace, which had fallen victim to a blaze in 1731.

Squares in Reims and Nancy served the architect as models for the rectangular, strictly symmetrical square with its magnificent palace and buildings, built using light-coloured stone in the style of Louis XVI. The square, despite all the traffic, is an intact, self-contained ensemble connected by archways. It accords splendid views of the lower city as well as serving as the perfect prelude to the Royal Palace that emerges behind it and the Parc de Bruxelles, also designed and built by Guimard.

Address Place Royale/Koningsplein, 1000 Brussels | Getting there Metro 1 or 5 to Gare Centrale/Centraal Station or Parc/Park or Metro 2 or 6 to Trône/Troon | Hours Accessible 24 hours | Tip On the east side of the square is the central tourist office. From here it is only a few metres to the Royal Museum of Fine Arts and the Magritte Museum.

55 La Bellone
The hidden baroque façade

La Bellone, the Maison du Spectacle or Het Huis van de Podiums-kunsten, can be visited at Rue de Flandre 46, if you can find it. Generally speaking, tourists walk straight past and have no idea what they're missing. Entering through what looks pretty much like a run-of-the-mill front door, you first walk down a long dark corridor. Only then does the view open out, and the spectacular façade of a baroque house becomes visible: La Bellone.

Since 1980 the house has served as a practise space and workshop for numerous artists. There is a large specialist library for the visual arts, work spaces and since 1995 the spacious roofed courtyard for music, dance and theatre performances. But above all it is the magnificent backdrop of the house that is so impressive.

It was originally part of a convent of the Sisters of Jericho, the current façade was its outer wall. The convent was later abandoned, and the house stood empty until 1680. In this year Olympia Mancini, the mistress of King Louis XIV of France, niece of Cardinal Mazarin and mother of Prince Eugene, was forced to flee France. She was suspected of poisoning. The lady, an established name in many a cloak-and-dagger novel, sought protection in what was then the Spanish Netherlands. Brussels granted it, for reasons quite obviously for the Belgians: Olympia was a beautiful woman and France was the enemy.

The originally austere renaissance façade was ornamented in a baroque fashion, giving it its current appearance. The architect and sculptor was probably Jean Cosyn (1646–1708), who had also designed two façades on Grand-Place: the King's House and the Wheelbarrow Guild House. Olympia died penniless in Brussels in 1708 and the Bellone was gradually forgotten – until the Centre for Visual Arts moved in here in 1980 and created the wonderful roofed courtyard 15 years later.

Address Rue de Flandre / Vlaamsesteenweg 46, 1000 Brussels, +32 (0)2 5133333, www.bellone.be | Getting there Metro 1 or 5 to Sainte-Cathérine / Sint-Katelijne or metro 3 or 4 to Bourse / Beurs | Hours Mon & Tue 9am–5pm, Wed–Fri 9am–7pm, Sat 2–5pm | Tip Rue de Flandre is popular due to its many different bars and restaurants. Le Pré Salé and Domaine de Lintillac come highly recommended.

56 L'Archiduc

Jazz bar with a special past

L'Archiduc is a bit like the doorway into the neighbourhood of Dansaert, which is now very trendy again. And L'Archiduc has somehow always been there, even though the pub hasn't always seen good times. At the weekend, it can get really full, especially if there's a live concert.

A certain Madame Alice founded L'Archiduc in 1937, an establishment in which, they say, bankers and brokers from the nearby stock exchange would meet their 'secretaries' in order to frolic in the private booths. The glass-and-iron door, as well as the doorbell next to it, are still from the time when music was played and drinks were served but the business model was a different one. L'Archiduc was discreet and wives were not permitted. In 1953, the Belgian jazz icon Stan Brenders took over the bar. Brenders, who had played with Django Reinhardt and Nat King Cole, sat here at his piano almost every night, to the great joy of the guests. The private booths disappeared, but the rest of the interior – from the small bar and the deep leather armchairs to the semi-circular balcony – was maintained in the Art Deco style of the 1930s. Famous musicians have jammed in the rather small room behind the turquoise coloured façade, the late and great Toots Thielemans of course, but also Miles Davis.

In 1985 Jean-Louis and Nathalie Hennart took over the bar and have continued the tradition ever since. The piano still stands in the middle of the room. If you dare and can play, you are welcome to use it. Live bands regularly perform, especially at weekends, and play, first and foremost, jazz. In this case, jazz is seen as anything that does not belong definitively to any other musical pigeonhole. In winter, there is also 'jazz after shopping' on Saturdays and 'round about five' on Sundays, each between five and seven o'clock in the evening. L'Archiduc is also well known for the quality of its drinks.

Address Rue Antoine Dansaert 6, 1000 Brussels, +32 (0)2 5120652, www.archiduc.net | Getting there Tram 3, 4 or 32 and bus 86 to Bourse/Beurs | Hours Daily 4pm–5am | Tip Another jazz bar, Music Village, is a few metres away at Rue des Pierres/Steenstraat 50, and for bigger concerts there is Ancienne Belgique and Beursschouwburg next to Bourse.

57__ The Lace-Making Paradise

Brussels lace as an exclusive rarity

That which is offered up as real lace these days is frequently machine made or has a relatively simple pattern or is invariably very expensive. Lace making is a difficult craft, which is more at home in museum villages than in real manufacture nowadays. The heyday of handmade Brussels lace, the 'queen of lace', was during the Baroque and Rococo periods. The only place for those wishing to admire lace now is the museum. In 1977, the Museum of Costume and Lace was established not far from the Grand-Place, in order to present the textile cultural treasures of the city of Brussels in the right light. The starting point of the collection was the inventory of vestments and laces that were stored in the Musée du Roi.

An especially fine thread, the prettiest motifs and perfect crafts-manship: all of this came together to make 18th-century 'Brussels lace' one of the most coveted goods in Europe. In this period, a good 10,000 workers made bonnets and bodices, ribbons, cuffs and whole dresses in Brussels alone. Roses and carnations, deer and dolphins, as well as religious scenes became textile images and helped their producers to what was relative prosperity at the time. Brussels lace was so sought-after that lace-makers were forbidden from leaving the country. At the same time, English producers tried to attract the women with free accommodation. The French Revolution put an end to the fashion for lace. The demand dried up abruptly, and at the same time tulle with appliquéd flowers was cheap and easy to produce. All that is left is the reputation and the term 'Brussels lace'.

In the 19th century the first machines that could produce similar textiles were invented. A layperson might not be able to tell whether lace is made by a machine or by hand straight away. But there are some clues: machines can't create round shapes, only braids and edges.

Address Musée du Costume et de la Dentelle, Rue de la Violette/Violetstraat 12, 1000 Brussels, +32 (0)2 2134450, www.costumeandlacemuseum.brussels/fr | **Getting there** Pedestrian zone, bus 48 or 95 to Parlement Bruxellois | **Hours** Tue–Sun 10am–5pm | **Tip** The majority of the shops that sell lace are to be found on Rue de l'Étuve/Stoofstraat, just round the corner from the museum. Manufacture Belge de Dentelles in Galerie du Roi/Koningsgalerij is more expensive and more classy.

58__ The Landmark
The window of the Maison Saint-Cyr

The painter Georges Léonard de Saint-Cyr (1854–1922) was, during his lifetime, a well-known man in Brussels. As an artist, he has largely been forgotten, but not as a building contractor. Showpiece of the numerous houses he had built, especially in the neighbourhood of Schaerbeek, is his private home on Square Ambiorix in today's European quarter.

Between 1901 and 1903, architect Gustave Strauven (1878–1919) created this gem on a plot that was only just four metres wide. Architects count the Art Nouveau house among the 500 most interesting structures in the world. This is not only due to its very narrow 'width' – the house really does attract the gaze of passersby. The picture is dominated by intricate wrought iron: beginning with the face facing the street, continuing in the studding and the balcony railings on all four floors and finding its conclusion in a roof crown. And then there's the window, that's actually not a window at all, but rather a circular opening in the upper floor with a loggia behind it. The window-eye dominates not only the house, but the whole street. A real landmark.

The house has often changed hands. The upkeep of this gem is expensive – renovations were already valued at more than 1.5 million euros in 1990. Despite its minimal width, the house comprises 370 square metres of living space. Due to its prominent location, the Saint-Cyr ultimately became an object of speculation. For a long time it was in danger of simply going to ruin. The house has been a listed building since 1988. The façade was renovated in 2008, subsidised by the City of Brussels for 370,000 euros, but we can only really speculate about what is going on inside. It is in private hands and isn't open to the public, but the current owner, an anonymous citizen of Brussels, recently applied to convert the Maison Saint-Cyr into a luxury B&B with only three suites.

Address Square Ambiorix 11, 1000 Brussels | Getting there Metro 1 or 5 to Schuman or bus 60, 63, 64 to Ambiorix (right in front of the house) | Hours Accessible 24 hours from the outside only | Tip The Avenue de la Brabançonne, which branches off from Square Ambiorix, is worth walking along. The avenue is lined on both sides with tall Chinese Chamaecyparis, a very unusual sight in Europe.

59 Le Cirio

The Art Nouveau café with unaltered flair

Tourist traps may well await some people right next to the Bourse, but the Le Cirio is not one of them. On the contrary. Although many tourists do enjoy the view, sun (if available) and drinks under the balcony and awning of the street café, you will mainly find locals sitting on the red velour benches inside. This is down to the classic Brussels brasserie-café flair as much as the food and drinks on offer: small snacks, bistro cuisine and typical dishes, such as the pot roast dish Carbonade flamande. It goes without saying that peanuts or savoury snacks come free with any beer you order.

Le Cirio doesn't only radiate tradition, it actually has it. And a house drink, the 'half-en-half', a 50/50 mixture of Champagne and white wine. The name of the drink, a Brussels rarity, is the same whether ordered in Flemish or French: une/een halfenhalf. There are various more or less plausible stories about its genesis. One of the most probable is that the drink dates back to a stockbroker, who couldn't afford all that Champagne any more after a rather unlucky day. The Le Cirio contends that Jacques Brel regularly drank halfenhalf here. Was he really a halfenhalf drinker? Who knows? He certainly would have fitted in with the ambience.

The Art Nouveau façade, the furnishings, the gilded pillars, the panelling, the bar and the mirrors are all from the year 1909 and designed by Brussels decorator Henri Coosemans. They are now protected by a preservation order. The house itself is even older: it was established in 1886 by Francesco Cirio (1836–1900) as an Italian restaurant.

Cirio, who was actually a tinned food manufacturer, ran restaurants in several European cities at the time, including Berlin. The only one left today is Le Cirio in Brussels. And one more thing: a quick look in the toilets is worthwhile. They house eau de cologne automats dating from 1909.

Address Rue de la Bourse / Beursstraat 18–20, 1000 Brussels, +32 (0)2 5121395 | Getting there Metro 3 or 4 or tram 32 to Bourse / Beurs | Hours Daily 10am–midnight | Tip The historical bar Greenwich from 1914, furnished in an Art Nouveau ambience is also highly recommended (Rue des Chartreux / Kartuizersstraat 7). Rue Chartreux and Place Saint-Gery are the party streets.

60__The Lift

The great glass elevator between uptown and downtown

The two parallel elevator booths overcome the 30-metre difference in altitude between the upper and lower parts of the city in a few seconds. Accordingly, they are constantly moving, transporting locals and tourists, cyclists, flaneurs and school children, in fact anyone who wishes to avoid the exhausting climb or descent. They are free to use. The booths are also made of glass, so they offer – from the parts that aren't covered in stickers or scratches – a wonderful view. The upper platform is often used as a viewing point itself, as is the stone balustrade of Place Poelaert, from where you can reach the lift. The Ascenseur des Marolles was built in 2001 on behalf of the Ministry of Communication and Infrastructure: a good place to start a visit to Brussels or to round one off at sunset.

The view is one reason, but the elevator also makes the fractions within Brussels manifest: at the top is the French-speaking, elegant upper town, at the bottom the Flemish downtown in its hardest form, the Marollen. Behind you is the huge Palace of Justice by Joseph Poelaert (namesake of the square and the reason that 'schieve architek' – crooked architect – is seen as an insult in Brussels to this day) and in front the visual axis along the border between up and down, the Rue de la Régence to Place des Palais. To the west, you have a view over the whole of the old town, from Midi via the Kapellekerk to the top of the Town Hall tower on Grand-Place. You can see the Koekelberg with the National Basilica and all the way to Laeken and the Atomium.

In the past, the edge between uptown and downtown marked the language barrier between French and Flemish and the change from royal to commoner Brussels. The kindness of the locals often deceives guests, but the language barrier still exists and misunderstanding between Flemings and Walloons, stirred up politically, is actually growing.

Address Place Poelaert, 1000 Brussels | Getting there Metro 2 or 6 to Louise / Louiza or tram 92 or 93 to Poelaert | Hours Accessible 24 hours | Tip Once you've alighted down in the Marollen, follow Rue Haute to the right to some expensive antique shops or to the left to the Museum Art & Marges (312–314), which exhibits art by autodidacts and outsiders.

61__The Loudspeaker

La Pasionaria – giving the people a voice

Brussels is the ultimate melting pot. People of different nationalities and social backgrounds live cheek by jowl. This is nowhere more striking than at Midi train station. Here business people on the way to the high-speed Thalys train to Paris or the Eurostar to London pass vendors of counterfeit Hèrmes bags or Africans looking for provisions from home in the cheap shops all around the station.

The Spanish-born Brussels artist Emilio López-Menchero installed his work of art right here, at the crossroads of Stalingrad and Midi. The oversized horn is a loudspeaker, four metres long, with an opening measuring 2.30 metres in diameter and made out of 10-millimetre-thick, polished stainless steel. Nine steps lead up to a platform, and everyone is invited to cry out in joy or anger, happiness or rage through the loudspeaker, sharing their emotions with the world. The art work is dedicated to all migrants. Its purpose is to give the people a voice.

The sculpture has a real-life role model. During the Spanish Civil War, a truck with a huge loudspeaker drove along the front line to motivate the soldiers in their fight against Franco's fascists. It broadcast speeches by Dolores Ibárruri, who was called La Pasionaria (the Passionflower). They always included her famous phrase 'No pasarán' – 'They shall not pass' – with the demand for all republicans to defend the country and Madrid. The film *The Spanish Earth* by the Dutch documentary filmmaker Joris Ivens features the truck. One of the writers and voice artists in the film was Nobel Prize for Literature-winner Ernest Hemingway.

La Pasionaria, which refers to this, was inaugurated in July 2006 on the 40th anniversary of Moroccan immigration to Belgium. Many Belgian demonstrations end at this square – when it becomes clear that the loudspeaker is almost as powerful as an electrically amplified megaphone.

Address Avenue Stalingrad 128, 1000 Brussels | **Getting there** Metro 2 or 6 to Gare de Midi / Zuidstation or tram 3, 4 or 32 to Lemonnier | **Hours** Accessible 24 hours | **Tip** On Friday evenings, Miguel Fernandez at El Rincon de España (Rue de l'Abbatoir / Slachthuisstraat 43) is the man to visit to hear authentic flamenco. Sometimes Miguel sings himself, and top-class Flamenco guitarists often play.

62 Maison Cauchie

A house as an advertising banner

Paul Cauchie (1875–1952) is certainly not the only painter to have designed their own home themselves. But his house is definitely unique.

The façade of the house is graphical and strictly linear and modelled on Charles Mackintosh's (1868–1928) Glasgow style. Unlike what was otherwise normal for Belgian Art Nouveau – the house was built in 1905 – it has no floral elements, and expensive materials such as marble or bluestone were not used. Instead it is a special plaster that looks like a canvas painted with large pictures in the style of the British Art Nouveau illustrator Aubrey Beardsley (1872–1898) that is captivating. It is actually what is known as *sgraffito*, a plaster and stucco technique, used in Italy since the Renaissance. The female figures around the round window in the upper storey symbolise architecture, fine art and the applied arts.

The house was a manifesto that exhibited the avant-garde art of Cauchie and his wife Caroline Voet (1875–1969), intended as an advertising measure for their collective work. The building was, on one hand, the artist couple's home and place of retreat – evident in the inscription 'par nous – pour nous' (by us – for us) on the façade picture of the first floor – but also their studio and sales exhibition. The two panels in the ground floor show what customers could order from the Cauchie company – from furniture and interiors to façade decoration.

After the death of Caroline Voet in 1969, this house was also almost torn down in favour of a new apartment building. The owners at the time, Guy and Leo Decissy, were able to purchase it and save it, literally at the last minute. The Tintin museum was supposed to move in here after elaborate renovations, but those plans were abandoned. And so the basement became a small museum, in which there is furniture and numerous other *sgraffito* works on display.

Address Rue des Francs/Frankenstraat 5, 1040 Brussels, +32 (0)2 7338684 | Getting there Tram 81, bus 22, 27, 61 or 80 to Merode | Hours First weekend of the month 10am–1pm & 2–5.30pm | Tip The former Hôtel Cohn-Donnay has been the home of the brasserie De Ultieme Hallucinatie since 1981. The pub owner Fred Dericks, who has since died, had bought and carefully restored the vacant 1904 Art Nouveau palace (Rue Royale/Koningsstraat 316).

63___The Mall

A key feature of the 19th century

Some will find the term 'shopping mall' irreverent, but that is what this beautiful luxury arcade was built to be. It is made up of two separate buildings, the Galleries of the King and the Queen. The passages, measuring 213 metres in total, are divided in the middle by a street. Each is a straight arcade with shops on both sides of the ground floor, and two more storeys on top, the upper floor reserved to this day for private apartments. Natural light shines in through the curved glass roof, at the time a tremendous innovation, both visually and technically. Together with the arcade in St Petersburg built one year earlier, the Galeries Royales Saint-Hubert in Brussels became a blueprint for the Galleria Vittorio Emanuele II in Milan and the GUM in Moscow, but also for all modern shopping palaces.

The Dutch architect Jean-Pierre Cluysenaar (1811–1880) had the idea of replacing the densely built up und highly disreputable section of the city centre around the herb market with a shopping street. In this way, downtown Brussels was to be made attractive for the 'upper social classes'. Cluysenaar and the banker Jean-André Demot founded the Société des Galeries Saint-Hubert in 1836. The project proved difficult and hung in the balance several times. The initiators had to negotiate for nine years in order to settle all the property rights in the quarter behind Grand-Place. The building work finally began in the spring of 1846.

Only one year later, in June 1847, King Leopold I opened the arcade personally, a real coup for the developers, who couldn't have dreamt of better advertising for their bold project. Brussels became chic overnight with its metropolitan flair. To this day, all of the city's big chocolatiers have their flagship stores here, as well as theatre shops, leather and fur shops, jewellers, the hatter Monsel and Brussels' oldest shop for lace.

Address Galerie du Roi / Koningsgalerij 5, 1000 Brussels | Getting there Metro 1 or 5 or bus 29, 38, 63, 65, 66 or 71 to Gare Centrale / Centraal Station, tram 92 or 93 or bus 27, 38, 71 or 95 to Royale | Hours Accessible 24 hours | Tip The film museum Cinematek at Rue Baron Horta 9 shows films in two auditoriums from an inventory of over 60,000 reels.

64 — Marcolini

When chocolate becomes art

Apologies to the Swiss and the French, but the best chocolate comes from Brussels. And the grand artist among the numerous Brussels chocolatiers is Pierre Marcolini. Neuhaus may have invented secure packaging for pralines and thus the business model with the 'Ballotin' in 1915, the Greek-born Leonidas Kestekides may make the biggest profits, Wittamer, Godiva and Galler may be more well known, but the benchmark in terms of quality and taste is set by Pierre Marcolini.

Born in 1964 in Charleroi as the son of Italian parents, Marcolini became aware of his passion for patisserie at an early age. He learned the trade under some of the greatest and was elected world champion in 1995. In the same year he opened his first shop in Brussels, radically changing the world of chocolate and patisserie. There were no bars on offer here – Marcolini presented works of art.

The display makes it look more like a jewellery shop, and like a Parisian fashion designer, there are two collections every year, in summer and in winter, the flavours fitting to the seasons. There are always new aromas and combinations. From pepper and jasmine to green or black tea, many things go well together with chocolate, if you know how and if you really produce the chocolate yourself from the most select ingredients. Marcolini travels all around the world looking for the best cacao and buys it directly from the grower. His motto: the best cacao beans can only be produced with great care, and that has its price. The same goes, of course, for his products. A square of chocolate costs 7.50 euros, a homemade ice cream with fresh chocolate coating, 3 euros.

Today, Marcolini has become a small chocolate empire with 350 employees and 30 shops all around the world, 8 of which are in Brussels. But the centrepiece remains the original shop in Rue des Minimes on the corner of Place du Grand Sablon.

Address Rue des Minimes / Miniemenstraat 1, 1000 Brussels, +32 (0)2 5141206, www.marcolini.com | **Getting there** Tram 92 or 93 to Petit Sablon or bus 27, 48 or 95 to Grand Sablon | **Hours** Mon–Thu & Sun 10am–7pm, Fri & Sat 10am–8pm | **Tip** In La Manufacture (Grand Sablon / Grote Zavel 39) you can watch the production of not so sweet works of art. Different, rawer, but also highly recommended are the pralines from Laurent Gerbaud at Rue Ravenstein 2d.

65 __ The Marionette Theatre
Puppets performing the Belgian Revolution

If you want to understand Brussels, and the Belgians in general, then visit Théâtre Toone – a good laugh is guaranteed too. The little stage is the heart and soul of the city. Right next to the Grand-Place and yet hidden in a backyard, two tiny alleyways lead to the two entrances, i.e. straight into the pub. Hand-carved rod puppets hang on the walls and there are painted theatre scenes in the alcoves. The Toone isn't a Punch and Judy show though, it's a theatre for adults. The repertoire includes more than 30 pieces: classics from Molière to Shakespeare, from opera to Goethe's *Faust*. But one thing it is never: deadly serious.

The Toone, now in its eighth generation of players, is the last puppet theatre of its kind. There used to be 60 of these adult-education establishments in Brussels; those who couldn't read found literature and education here. People who would otherwise be cold at home threw their few pieces of coal together on the communal fire and watched an act every evening. Not too long or too complicated, so there was time after to sit around the fire. Themes were presented with a sense of humour – the audience already had enough problems – in the Brussels dialect so that everyone understood the content. Today the programme states 'Français, Nederlands, Deutsch, English and Espagnol'; in fact, these languages are simply thrown together – basically the Brussels dialect. And the small museum that serves as refreshment hall in the interval has retained the original authentic ambience.

It is most 'Brusselsy' when the Belgian Revolution is performed. Loud and colourful, it features Eddy Merckx, the son of the devil, and *Manneken Pis* of course. In the end, many things are explained more clearly than in the clever history books. And there are a couple of jokes about the king thrown in too – the locals like nothing better than laughing at themselves.

Address Théâtre Toone, Marché aux Herbes / Grasmarkt 66 (Impasse Pétronille) and Petite Rue des Bouchers / Korte Beenhouwersstraat (Impasse Schuddeveld 6), 1000 Brussels, www.toone.be | Getting there Metro 1 or 5 to Gare Centrale / Centraal Station; Théâtre Toone is in a pedestrian zone | Hours Shows begin Thu–Sat 8.30pm, plus Sat 4pm; reservations: +32 (0)2 5117137 | Tip The courtyard in front of the theatre is a lively place to eat and drink.

66 __ The Martyr Square
Urban rectangle without all the fuss and clamour

What a beautiful square, a gem – and yet hardly given the time of day by the general public: laid out symmetrically in the Neo-Classical style between 1774 and 1778, following the designs of architect and engineer Claude Fisco (1736 – 1825) and surrounded by luxurious white buildings in the architectural style of Louis XVI. On top of that, it is a square steeped in history, a place for the dead and for martyrs.

This refers to the events of the year 1830, the September days of the Belgian Revolution. The mood among the general population towards the occupying Dutch forces had been vehemently angry for a long time. Following the performance of the historical opera *La Muette de Portici* by Daniel-François-Esprit Auber in the Brussels Opera on 25 August, this anger was vented. The touchpaper had been lit: Vive la liberté! Buildings were destroyed and plundered, factories occupied, the Belgian flag hoisted.

The situation got out of control and the uprising was countered violently. Hundreds of Belgians met their deaths in the ensuing street clashes. Some 450 'Heroes of the Belgian Revolution' were shot in the barricade battles in the city centre and ultimately buried beneath a crypt in the middle of the Martyr Square.

The memorial in the middle of the square is dedicated to those killed in the revolution. The 'Patria' with the Belgian lion, who bursts the chains of suppression, and the four weeping women on its plinth, was created in 1836 according to designs by the architect Louis Roelandt (1786 – 1864). The sculptor Guillaume Geefs (1805 – 1883) added the sculptures and haunting marble reliefs with scenes from the revolution in a walk-through area below the level of the square two years later. Henry van de Velde erected a memorial to the leader of the revolution Louis-Fréderic de Merode in an Art Nouveau style on the south side of the square.

Address Place des Martyrs/Martelarenplein, 1000 Brussels | Getting there Metro 3 or 4 to De Brouckère, metro 2 to Rogier or tram 3, 52, 55, 56 or 81 to De Brouckère | Hours Accessible 24 hours | Tip Théâtre des Martyrs is at Place des Martyrs 22 (+32 (0)2 2233208). The irony of history: Ministers of the Flemish regional government have installed their luxurious cabinets in some of these historic buildings, which represent Belgium as a state.

67 Matongé
Kinshasa in the centre of Brussels

Africa begins at the Porte de Namur, or more accurately, Matongé. The lively neighbourhood in the shadow of the EU's modern buildings in the centre of Brussels is named after a district of Kinshasa, the capital of the Democratic Republic of Congo. All the shops in Matongé resound with African rhythms; cassava, plantains and yams are laid out on display; everywhere you go there are colourful fashions and hair salons offering braids, dreads and other African hairstyles; while telephone shops offer cheap tariffs for calls to Accra, Abidjan or Dakar.

The Congolese, however, were not permitted to travel to Belgium until 1958. The first to come were a choir from Kinshasa, invited to take part in the World's Fair – the African guests were taken care of on behalf of the authorities by the aristocrat Dame Monique van der Straten. As a farewell, she stated: 'Those who wish to study here are more than welcome'. That was to be the starting point of a new era. In the first year, it was 8, then 20, then several hundred potential students who van der Straten was charged with accommodating. To this end she founded the Africa House, a cultural centre in Matongé and residence for 72 students to this day. The Maison Africaine became the nucleus of the neighbourhood. The proportion of academically educated people in the African community continues to be above average, but not, however, their social standing or income.

As well as Congolese, people from numerous states in sub-Saharan Africa came later. Many no longer live in the triangle of Chaussée de Wavre, Rue de la Tulipe and Chaussée d'Ixelles. But no matter how many times it is written off, Matongé still remains the meeting place. The Galeries d'Ixelles are at its centre. Written above its two doors (they are called Kinzia and Kanda Kanda after two other neighbourhoods in Kinshasa): 'Smile, you're in Matongé'.

Address Triangle Chaussée de Wavre/Waversesteenweg, Rue de la Tulipe and Chaussée d'Ixelles, 1000 Brussels | **Getting there** Metro 2 or 6 or bus 34, 54 or 80 to Porte de Namur/Naamsepoort | **Hours** Accessible 24 hours | **Tip** The memorial *Beyond Hope* by the Congolese artist Freddy Tsimba from 2007 is at Chaussée de Wavre 59. Made up of oversized spent cartridges, it is intended to draw attention to the fate of child soldiers. Horloge du Sud is recommended for eating and listening to music (Rue du Trône/Troonstraat 141).

68__ The Memorial

Le Messager commemorates those murdered
by Marc Dutroux

When you walk into the large, picturesque Parc de Bruxelles, situated between the Royal Palace and the parliament building, you are usually greeted with the same image: joggers, children playing, lovers walking hand in hand. A relaxed atmosphere in the 1774 geometric city oasis, surrounded by numerous sculptures – Greek gods, Roman emperors, legendary figures – around the expansive fountain and along the partially covered paths.

And then, on the side of the classical Palais de Nation (home of the parliament and the senate in the northwest corner of the park, built between 1779 and 1783), near a children's playground, the visitor comes across a two-metre-high bronze statue of a very different kind. An opened hand lets a bird fly free. Written on the plinth in various languages: 'The Messenger – For the lost children'. The memorial commemorates one of the darker chapters in Belgium's recent history, which caused horror around the world and at times left Belgium paralysed: the crimes and murders of Marc Dutroux and his accomplices, who had kidnapped, abused and murdered several children, which came to light in the middle of the 1990s. And time and again the suggestion that the child abusers had confidants and cronies right up into the country's highest political and juridical circles. One thing was certain: the rival police and judicial authorities had failed across the board.

Le Messager was created in 1997 on the initiative of the daily paper *La Libre Belgique* by the Brussels graphic artist, painter and sculptor Jean-Michel Folon (1934–2005). King Albert and Queen Paola were among those in attendance at the unveiling of the memorial. At the same time, a few metres away, the parliamentary commission of inquiry of the Dutroux case was in session, which on this day was about the complicity of politics and justice in this jungle of foul play.

Address Parc de Bruxelles (between Palais de la Nation / Parlament and Palais Royal), 1000 Brussels | **Getting there** Metro 1 or 5 to Parc / Park or tram 92 or 94 to Palais or Parc / Park | **Hours** Accessible 24 hours | **Tip** Théâtre Royal du Parc, built in 1782, is in the northeast part of the park. A trip to Fondation Folon in Parc Solvay, where the artist is acknowledged with his own museum, is also worthwhile (Drève de la Ramée 6/A, 1310 La Hulpe).

69_ The Memorial Wall
The attack on 22 March, 2016

A normal Tuesday morning in Brussels: it's rush hour at Brussels Airport, with take-offs and landings every few minutes. In the city centre, throngs of people hurry to work. Maelbeek metro station, in the middle of the European quarter, is equally busy.

At a few minutes before eight, two explosive devices go off in the departure hall within a few seconds of each other. The glass front of the hall smashes, parts of the ceiling fall in. People are killed, injured, in a state of panic. Two suicide bombers have blown themselves up and taken a dozen others with them to their deaths, over 100 air travellers are injured, some fatally. And then, a few minutes after nine o'clock, a second suicide attack in Brussels city centre – in Maelbeek metro station, not far from the European Parliament and the European Council. This time the explosion takes place in the middle carriage of a stationary metro train. The station is engulfed in an inferno, the dead and injured in the confinement of the underground; there is shock and horror.

A little later the full extent of the catastrophe becomes clear. The attacks, for which the terrorist organisation 'Islamic State' claim responsibility, cost 35 people their lives, with over 300 injured. Brussels is in a state of emergency, public transport is suspended, the airport closed. The city is shrouded in deep sorrow – statements of solidarity, candles, a sea of flowers.

A large billboard in the entrance halls of Maelbeek metro station – written and painted on by family and friends of the victims, in the middle of which a touching red heart is open for any other thoughts – is a commemoration of the horrors of 22 March, 2016. Many stop for a moment, turning their thoughts to the people affected, perhaps writing their own thoughts on the wall. After all, this treacherous attack could have hit any of those who hurry past here every day.

Address Maelbeek metro station, Rue de la Loi/Wetstraat, 1000 Brussels | Getting there Metro 1/5 to Maelbeek, exit Rue de la Loi | Hours Accessible 24 hours | Tip There is another commemorative plaque on the outside of Maelbeek metro station – with a text by the successful Belgian author Griet Op de Beeck.

70 Moeder Lambic

30 beers on tap at any one time

Simply ordering a beer at Moeder Lambic is a bit like going into a bookshop and saying 'I'd like a book please'. You're going to have to be a bit more specific, as there are more than 100 types here and a couple of beer cocktails on top. Light or dark, cloudy or clear, bitter or rather sweet, normal, strong or really strong, bottle fermentation or from the cask, from Brussels, Belgium or even from abroad, craft beer or large brewery – the range on offer is overwhelming. There's a beer menu, which offers a daily and weekly selection, but more impressively, there are always 30 different beers available fresh from the cask.

In order to make the drinker's confusion complete, not only does every sort of beer have its own, often very idiosyncratically shaped glass, there are also several pubs named Moeder Lambic. The pub name has a bit of a tradition in Brussels. The first Chez Moeder Lambic, from the beginning of the 20th century, was in Bois de la Cambre on the edge of town, but it burned down in 1975. The second opened at the start of the 1980s in Saint-Gilles. This is where the tradition of serving several different beers was established. The beer menu weighed a good two kilogrammes. Unfortunately, some of the bottled beer was also a little bit past its drink-by date.

In 2006, the current proprietor took over the pub and immediately established a second one. Large, modern and stylish, the Moeder Lambic on Place Fontainas in the city centre is more a place for drinking. Chez Moeder Lambic in Saint-Gilles, on the other hand, is small and original. Both follow the concept that various tastes and situations call for different beers. You wouldn't just have one type of wine on your menu, would you? In Belgium, each has its own story. Ask the bartender. And don't forget: many Belgian beers are stronger than your run-of-the-mill lager, some significantly so.

Address Rue de Savoie 68, 1060 Brussels (Saint-Gilles/Sint-Gillis), +32 (0)2 5441699, www.moederlambic.com | Getting there Tram 81 or 97 or bus 48 to Barrière | Hours Daily 4pm–3am | Tip In Malting Pot at Rue Scarron/Scarron-Straat 50 you buy the beer by the bottle – the right beer for every taste and every mood. A crate of just one sort would be sacrilege and a betrayal of the many other possibilities.

71 The Monument to Labour
The nomadic history of the Monument au Travail

The Monument to Labour stands right next to the Charleroi–Antwerp canal, on the northern edge of the large Vergote dock: large, powerful and monumental. The harbour and a workers' memorial – you would be forgiven for thinking they belong together. But the monument was never supposed to be here.

Constantin Meunier (1831–1905), an important Belgian naturalist sculptor, created the five statues and four reliefs between 1890 and 1900. The latter depict people at work and simultaneously symbolise the four elements: industry (fire), steelworkers at work; mining (earth), miners at the coalface; the harvest (air), farmers harvesting; and finally, the harbour (water) with the dock workers. The statues are called *Motherhood* (symbol of the future), *Ancestor* (past), *Sower* (production) as well as *Miner* and *Smith* (coal and steel). Originally, they were to be mounted as a semi-circle or pyramid – Meunier was a freemason. This and its location were the subject of many discussions. The monument was originally to be erected on the roundabout on Avenue Tervuren for Meunier's 70th birthday in 1901. However, the government forbade this; there was no way they were going to create a place of pilgrimage and demonstration for the socialists. A Dane offered to erect the work in Denmark, which led to such public protest that the government ended up buying it in 1902 without having a place to display it. After Meunier's death, the individual parts were on show for a short time in 1909. In 1926, the Belgian architectural association announced a competition with the aim of finally installing the monument. The architect Mario Knauer was awarded the contract in 1929, and in the following year the monument was erected in its current form, though not in its current location in Laeken. It made the jump across the harbour basin from Jules de Trooz square in Schaerbeek in 1954.

Address Quai des Yachts, Grand Bassin Vergote, 1020 Brussels (Laeken) | Getting there
Tram 62 or 93 to Outre Ponts or bus 57 to Claessens | **Hours** Accessible 24 hours | Tip
A number of the artist's sculptures and pictures are presented in Musée Meunier, his former
home (Rue de L'Abbaye / Abdijstraat 59, Brussels-Ixelles).

72__ The MOOF
At the altar of the Smurfs

Even from the outside, it is clear at first sight what the MOOF, the Museum of Original Figurines, is all about. Five metres high and weighing over 900 kilos, a shiny white Smurf stands right in front of the entrance. It was erected on 25 June, 2012, the birthday of the Belgian illustrator Peyo, born Pierre Culliford (1928–1992), inventor of the small blue creatures.

Behind the giant Smurf is the biggest fan shop in the world for 'Les Schtroumpfs', as they are called in the original. In the building to the left, which is also the entrance to the metro in Galerie Horta, an escalator leads down to the basement.

The MOOF was founded in 2011 as intentional competition to the state Musée de la Bande Dessinée. It isn't a museum in the proper sense, but rather an expression of fandom.

Over 3,000 square metres, the founder and boss, Eric Pierre, has brought together comic figures in every imaginable size to create scenes from the strips. There are rooms for all the famous figures created by Belgian illustrators, not only the Schtroumpfs/Smurfs. You will find Gaston Lagaffe, Spirou and Marsupilami, Lucky Luke, Michel Vaillant, Tintin and Milou, and all the others too. And because, according to his creators Uderzo and Goscinny, he is first and foremost a European, Asterix, his friend Obelix and a 'real' magic pot also make an appearance. A small cinema area awaits fans who have some time on their hands. Here animated films are screened in their original length of 70 minutes (*The Smurfs*, *Tintin*, *Asterix* and *Lucky Luke*). The language can be changed on request at the entrance.

Peyo actually created the Smurfs in 1958 as supporting roles for his favourite character Pirlouit, in English 'Peewit'. They soon got their own album and a series on American television followed, which ended up making the little blue men famous all around the world.

Address Galerie Horta, Rue Marché aux Herbes / Grasmarkt 116, 1000 Brussels, +32 (0)2 2077992, www.moofmuseum.be | **Getting there** Metro 1 or 5 or tram 92, 93 or 94 to Gare Centrale / Centraal Station | **Hours** Thu–Sun 10am–6pm, Tue & Wed reserved for groups | **Tip** Fans and collectors of other figures will find a number of shops in Brussels, the biggest selection being in Boutique Tintin at Rue de la Colline / Heuvelstraat 13.

73__ The Murals

Paul Delvaux in the Bourse/Beurs metro station

There can't be many places in a metropolis that are more highly frequented than underground stations. This is one of the reasons that many cities have decided to decorate their underground stations, to breathe atmosphere into them, to furnish them with art. But no European city is as experimental and consistent in this as Brussels. Metro stations as a location of contemporary art – this has been a tradition in Brussels for many decades. Murals, sculptures, mosaics and photographs furnish almost all of the 69 stations of the Brussels metro network with their very own character. You will find them in the entrance halls, before escalators take you underground, then in the stations themselves, where you can also sneak a peek when passing through aboard a train. The Brussels metro is an underground art gallery.

Alongside René Magritte, one of the most important surrealists among the artists based in Brussels in the 20th century was Paul Delvaux (1897–1994). He created a nostalgic street scene focused on the tramways of yore for the station under the Brussels stock exchange in 1978. *Nos Vieux Trams Bruxellois* (*Our Old Brussels Trams*) is a view of the old, street-level transportation system. Also on display in Bourse station is a ceiling installation by the painter and sculptor Pol Bury (1922–2005).

Hankar station is adorned with an oversized mural by Roger Somville (1923–2014) from the year 1976, *Notre Temps* (*Our Time*). The work *Sept Écritures* (*Seven Scripts*) from 1976 by the Belgian painter Pierre Alechinsky (born 1927) and Christian Dotremont (1922–1979), who both belonged to the avant-garde artist group Cobra in the 1950s, can be admired in Anneessen. The artist Benoît van Innis single-handedly repaired his cartoon-like tiled artwork in Maelbeek station, which had been damaged in the deadly attack on a metro train in March 2016.

Address Rue Henri Maus 2, Place de la Bourse, 1000 Brussels | Getting there Metro 3 or 4 or tram 31 or 32 to Bourse/Beurs | Hours Around the clock (a day ticket is highly recommended) | Tip You should definitely take a look at the Bourse, Brussels' stock exchange, up on street-level, built between 1868 and 1873 by Léon Suys. The French sculptor Auguste Rodin lived in Brussels on several occasions and was involved in the design of the sculptures at the Bourse in 1870.

74 Musée Wiertz

A studio built to the paintings' dimensions

This museum is special to Brussels. The 16-metre-high studio, with its slightly tapering glass roof, is second to none. Such an unusual space was necessary for the artist to be able to succeed in his undertaking: to paint pictures on the scale of those by Rubens and Michelangelo, whom he emulated.

The history painter Antoine Wiertz (1806–1865) was a favourite of King Leopold I of Belgium. He admired him as the master of Belgian Romanticism and granted him his numerous extravagances. Leopold wanted his protégé to stick to this kind of painting, even though the pieces, often oversized, were difficult to sell. This demanded a practical solution. The king decreed that the artist be built a home and studio house in Ixelles at public expense, in which he could produce his large-format pictures with religious and philosophic-allegoric scenes. They certainly corresponded to the zeitgeist and were, despite any artistic contention, extremely popular.

The atelier was built at such a grand size –16 metres high, 35 metres long and 15 metres wide – so that the works could be accommodated. The condition of this deal was that the residential and studio house should pass over to Belgian state ownership after the death of the artist. The building, realised in 1850 according to the designs of the painter himself, was converted into a museum after his death in 1865 and is now a branch of the Royal Museums of Fine Arts.

To this day, the pictures and paintings on display in the atelier museum are exclusively those of Antoine Wiertz, in total around 220 works. This includes the over-five-metre-high and eight-metre-wide painting *The Greeks and the Trojans Fighting over the Body of Patroclus*, but also *The Premature Burial and La Belle Rosine*, in which the half-naked Rosine stands face to face with a skeleton. Several sculptures are also exhibited.

Address Musée Wiertz Museum, Rue Vautier 62, 1050 Brussels (Ixelles/Elsene), +32 (0)2 6481718, www.fine-arts-museum.be | Getting there Metro 1 or 5 to Maelbeek and Schuman or bus 34 or 80 to Museum | Hours Tue–Fri 10am–noon & 12.45–5pm | Tip In front of the Royal Academies for Science and the Arts at Rue Ducale/Hertog-straat 1 (Academy Palace), not far from the city palace, a pair of glasses with narrow frames is embedded in an illuminated cobblestone on the square – a real eye-catcher.

75__ The NATO Star
Fenced in and behind bars

Considering the fact that the NATO star is one of the best known symbols in the world, there is relatively little known about its genesis. The reason for this is that the corresponding documents were destroyed when NATO's headquarters moved from Paris to Brussels in 1966/1967.

In 1951, the diplomat Lester Bowles Pearson (1897–1972), at the time foreign minister, later Prime Minister of Canada, suggested that NATO be furnished with a symbol. One year later, in 1952, a competition to create an emblem for the alliance was announced. The winning suggestion was submitted by a member of the international staff, but unfortunately their name can no longer be ascertained. The design is a four-pointed compass needle, white on blue, with two short (north and south) and two longer (east and west) lines extending from the tips. This compass rose was intended to symbolise NATO's comprehensive scope. In 1969, NATO decided to make Brussels its permanent headquarters. To this end, they looked for a powerful symbol for the commemorative courtyard in front of the building and ultimately chose a design by the Belgian architect Raymond Huyberechts. It envisaged the creation of a seven-metre-tall steel sculpture of the NATO star, penetrated by two circles. The compass rose symbolises the aspiration of international involvement, the two circles, offset from each other by 90 degrees, stand for the transatlantic pact between Europe and America. The statue, which cost 1.5 million Belgian francs, was erected in the middle of August 1971 and inaugurated one month later. The Dutchman Joseph Luns (1911–2002) was the first Secretary General of NATO to be photographed in front of the star, which has since become one of the most filmed symbols in the world. In 2016, the NATO headquarters relocated, from one side of the street to the other, taking the star with it.

Address Rue Léopold III, 1130 Brussels (Evere) | **Getting there** Tram 62 or bus 178, 272 or 471 to NATO/Navo | **Hours** Visible through the fence | **Tip** Almost 10 kilometres to the south you can see defence technology from the year 1300, in Kastell Beersel. The moated castle defended Brussels until 1540.

76__New De Wolf
The year-round market of fun

Locals walk through the Marollen to look for antiques and furniture, Rue Haute one way and Rue Blaes on the way back. Here there is one shop after the other, from Art Deco to Bauhaus to 1950s' styles. Shabby chic could have been invented here, so harmoniously do the houses, surroundings and goods on offer fit together.

In the middle of it all, at number 91, is New De Wolf. It has furniture and lamps too, but in particular decorative articles of all kinds; fabrics, lanterns, table and room decorations for every possible, as well as every impossible, occasion. If it can be placed on a table, a windowsill or a sideboard, or can be hung on the wall, the ceiling or a tree, you will find it in New De Wolf. The rooms, spread over two storeys, are literally overflowing. No motto is too bizarre, no theme too absurd – if it is illuminated jellyfish you're looking for, this would be the place you might find them.

Since July 1986, Susanne De Wolf has been in her shop 362 days a year, selling an unbelievable range of products. If you ask her why and about her motivation, she only says: 'It's just how I am' and 'I enjoy it'.

There are decoration ideas for every occasion and every time of year, from Easter or autumn, to children's birthday parties or themed adult parties. But New De Wolf really comes into its own in October, when it is time to ring in Christmas. The display window bursts at the seams, the whole shop is an endless range of Father Christmases, angels, pinecones, snowmen and snowwomen, baubles, reindeer and sledges and the most surprising range of things you could use to decorate a Christmas tree. Then, there's no other way to put it, all hell breaks out.

Apropos: candles aren't everyday items in Belgium and are actually quite hard to come by. This is not the case in New De Wolf. Here candles are a decoration for life, not just for Christmas.

Address Rue Haute / Hoogstraat 91, 1000 Brussels, +32 (0)2 5111018, www.newdewolf.be |
Getting there Bus 27 or 48 to La Chapelle | Hours Mon–Sat 10.30am–6.30pm, Sun
10am–5pm | Tip La vaisselle au kilo is almost directly opposite. The name says it all.
Kitchen utensils, glasses, cutlery and crockery are no longer – like in the old location at
Sablon – sold by weight, but still at very moderate prices.

77__The Opera
High art and the Belgian Revolution

La Monnaie / De Munt has written history. It is 25 August, 1830. On the programme of the Brussels opera house Théâtre de La Monnaie is the Belgian première of the patriotic opera *La Muette de Portici* by composer Daniel-François-Esprit Auber (1782–1871) with libretto by Eugène Scribe.

The story involves the revolt by Neapolitan fishermen against the authorities. Sitting in the royal box is King William I of The Netherlands. When rebellion against a restorative social order and foreign rule is called for in the name of the 'sacred love of the Fatherland' in the second act, thus citing the Marseillaise, and finally an aria calls for vengeance and the forcible liberation of the oppressed in the third act, the electrified Brussels opera audience can no longer contain themselves.

People storm out of the theatre, shouting 'to arms!' and rush to occupy the Palace of Justice. It is the beginning of the Belgian Revolution of 1830 and ultimately the ousting of the Dutch.

The opera – built in 1817 as the successor of a theatre opened in the year 1700 in place of the old 15th-century mint and already legendary in its time – fell victim to a blaze in 1855 and burned down completely but for the Neo-Classical pillared façade. The Belgian architect Joseph Poelaert (1817–1879) was responsible for the reconstruction of La Monnaie with its extravagant auditorium, based on the French theatre in the style of Louis XVI, and magnificent foyer. Modern auxiliary facilities were added in the 1980s.

La Monnaie remains a music theatre of worldwide repute to this day. The opera experienced artistically triumphant years between 1967 and 1987 under the French choreographer Maurice Béjart and his dance company 'Ballet of the 20th Century', with which he also wrote history and set the highest of standards. Béjart is now considered the great innovator of classical ballet.

Address Place de la Monnaie / Muntplein, 1000 Brussels, +32 (0)2 22291200, www.lamonnaie.be | **Getting there** Metro 1 or 5 to De Brouckère or tram 3, 4, 31 and 32 to Place de Monnaie | **Hours** Sightseeing tours Sept–June Sat noon; tickets Tue–Fri noon–6pm, Sat 10am–6pm | **Tip** Why not take a look inside the casino Viage at Boulevard Anspach 30, especially as there is much more entertainment on offer than a ball rolling around a roulette table.

78__Parc Josaphat
The Central Park of Schaerbeek

Twenty hectares of green in the style of an English landscaped garden: the northern end of Parc Josaphat borders the European quarter almost directly. However, you are not likely to meet any diplomats or EU officials here, unless they live in the pretty but not so fashionable neighbourhood of Schaerbeek.

The Belgian landscape architect Edmond Gallopin (1851–1919) created the current park in 1904 on behalf of the king. However, its history is older: in the Middle Ages this was the valley of a small stream called the Roodenbeek. As legend has it, a pilgrim from the Holy Land, gripped by the sight, said that it looked like the Valley of Josaphat near Jerusalem. And thus the name was given. In 1574, a votive column with this story was erected in the park on the so-called 'holy hill', but this was destroyed in 1793 during the French Revolution. Schaerbeek city council planned the park in the 1890s, but initially failed to realise it due to the resistance of a wealthy widow who owned parts of the site. She found the price offered so shockingly low that she threatened to fell all the trees on her land. So King Leopold II dispossessed her and commissioned the park.

Today joggers and parents with pushchairs do circuits of the hilly site. People enjoy the sun, and practise yoga or t'ai chi on the grassy areas around the lakes. There is a playground and a petting zoo for children, where the mascots of the park live: two donkeys called Camille and Gribouille. Concerts regularly take place in the music pavilion and there are two archery clubs. In autumn, you can watch the two powerful Ardennes draught horses Taram and Vouziers clearing wood. On the last Sunday in June, the park celebrates the 'cherry festival' (La Fête des Cerises) with lots of music. Sure, New York's Central Park is almost 20-times bigger, but the residents of Schaerbeek are proud of their Parc Josaphat.

Address Boulevard Lambermont, 1030 Brussels (Schaerbeek/Schaarbeek) | **Getting there**
Tram 7 to Chazal/Héliotropes/Louis Bertrand or bus 64, 65 or 66 to Chazal | **Hours**
Accessible 24 hours | **Tip** Dudenpark in the neighbourhood of Forest/Vorst is also very
pretty. If you climb from the lowest point at the Union Saint-Gilloise stadium to the
highest point, you'll be rewarded with a beautiful view over Brussels: the park is at a higher
altitude than the rest of the city.

79 __ The Parlamentarium

The EU Parliament presents itself to its citizens

For many, the European Union is alien and remote, some even reject it without ever having understood it. It is rebuked as a bureaucratic monster, far away from people's realities, but also admired as the guarantor of a democratic, peaceful post-war Europe. As ever, if knowledge about an institution and its content is vague and hard to grasp, taking a closer look is worthwhile, to gain information, get a look behind the scenes, in order to finally uncover the unknown. Once you have visited the Parlamentarium, the European Parliament's visitor centre, you will understand the function and workings of this widely ramified institution, and the point and duties of the European Union will be clearer. And just how international the EU is becomes evident in the 24 different languages used by 500 million EU citizens, and in which the Parlamentarium can be experienced. Where else in the world would you find something like this? Individual portable multimedia guides will lead you through the cleverly designed interactive exhibition.

You can take a virtual journey through Europe and the individual countries, or enter the 'Tunnel of Voices' to grasp how multilingual Europe really is (all bills and rulings by parliamentarians and politicians must be translated into 24 official languages).

In a 360-degree panorama film, the visitor has a realistic experience of the workings of the parliament. A walk-through European map invites you to explore the EU virtually on dozens of interactive terminals. The history and integration of Europe as well as questions and future challenges are discussed, and you can also get to know your representative from the 750 members of parliament.

The Parlamentarium, designed by the Stuttgart-based Atelier Brückner across 3,000 square metres of exhibition space, opened in 2001 after a four-year construction period at a cost of 21 million euros.

Address Bâtiment Willy Brandt, Esplanade Solidarnosc 1980, Rue Wiertz 60, 1047 Brussels, +32 (0)2 2832222 | **Getting there** Metro 1 or 5 to Maelbeek, metro 2 or 6 to Trône/Troon or bus 22, 27, 34, 38, 64, 80 or 95 to European Parliament | **Hours** Mon 1–6pm, Tue–Fri 9am–6pm, Sat & Sun 10am–6pm | **Tip** During the week, the adjoining Place du Luxembourg serves as a hip location with numerous restaurants and bars for a young, international and party-loving crowd.

80 — The Pavilion

Naked in Jubelpark

There are two buildings that stand directly next to one another in the northwest corner of Parc du Cinquantenaire/Jubelpark – and they couldn't be more contrasting if they tried. The large mosque, built in 1880 by Ernest van Humbeek as an oriental pavilion for the first Brussels World's Fair, and a smaller temple, at first glance classical in style, the so-called Horta-Lambeaux Pavilion. The pavilion was the first work of architecture by Victor Horta, built in 1896 to exhibit a twelve-by-eight-metre marble relief by the Belgian sculptor Jef Lambeaux (1852–1908) called *Human Passions*.

Reactions to the work were certainly passionate too and degenerated into outrage. 'Immoral' and 'obscene' were the mildest of characterisations. With it Lambeaux presents the stages of human life, accurate in every detail and full of power: birth, love, conflict and death. All the people in it are naked. And nakedness was not the only problem – the representation of Jesus on the cross above the other figures was seen as blasphemous. The building stayed like that, in its original condition, with an unobstructed view of the relief, for exactly three days. First a wooden fence was put up around the building, then the sides were bricked up, and finally the front entrance was closed off with large doors.

In 1967, the Belgian King Baudouin offered King Faisal of Saudi Arabia the oriental pavilion, so that he could establish a mosque there, in return for generous oil supplies. He overlooked, whether intentionally or not, that the Temple of Human Passions was also part of the site.

In 1976 it, together with the completely preserved relief, was bought back. It was renovated in 2006 and can be viewed during the summer time for one hour every day. Then the life-size marble figures wrestle, dance and love each other again, right next to the mosque of the Wahhabi World Muslim League.

Address Parc du Cinquantenaire/Jubelpark, 1000 Brussels | Getting there Metro 1 or 5 or tram 22, 27, 61, 80 or 91 to Merode | Hours Only in summer, tickets from MRAH (Royal Museum for Art and History), in the corner of the park diagonally opposite. Opening times can also be requested on +32 (0)2 7417215 | Tip There are numerous boules courts open to the public right next to the pavilion. They are highly frequented by pétanque players of very differing skill levels.

81 The Photo

Albert Einstein and Madame Curie in Métropole

If you aren't already staying in the classy hotel, then a visit to the Art Nouveau bar of the richly historical, five-star hotel Métropole built in 1895 is definitely worthwhile. Two brothers of the Wielemans family, owners of a brewery, had opened Café Métropole in 1890 in order to sell their beer in the city centre. They ultimately purchased the neighbouring bank building and had the luxury hotel with its Corinthian columns, coloured, curved windows, the impressive stucco ceiling and crystal chandeliers built by Belgian-French architect Alban Chambon (1847–1928). Parts of the former bank are integrated into the magnificent foyer. The bar was added, with lots of marble, stucco, palm trees and large mirrors. Bianca Jagger, Maurice Béjart, the racing car driver Jackie Stewart and even the conductor Arturo Toscanini way back in 1919 have immortalised their names on a plaque, mounted on a column decorated in gold.

But as if that wasn't enough, there is a very special photograph to be discovered on the edge of the foyer. An illustrious party of high-ranking scientists, almost all of them Nobel Prize winners, can be seen here on a group photo that was taken in the grand Hotel Métropole on the occasion of the first so-called Solvay Conference from 30 October to 3 November, 1911. The Belgian industrial magnate Ernest Solvay (1838–1922) had invited the scientific elite to this conference in Brussels in order to discuss the fundamental problems of contemporary physics research. The theme defined for the 18 physicists from seven different nations was 'The Theory of Radiation and Quanta'; they analysed the various approaches of the nascent quantum theory. Among them Walther Nernst, Max Planck and the young Albert Einstein. The star of this historic event and the only woman present was Marie Curie, double Nobel Prize winner in physics and chemistry.

CONSEIL DE PHYSIQUE SOLVAY
BRUXELLES 1911
HOTEL METROPOLE.

Address Hotel Métropole, Place de Brouckère/De Brouckèreplein 31, 1000 Brussels, +32 (0)2 2172300, www.metropolehotel.com | Getting there Metro 3 or 5 to De Brouckère | Hours The photo can be viewed during the hotel's opening hours. | Tip Boulevard Anspach has been completely car-free since 2016. You can walk along this new pedestrian zone to Place Fontainas and then Place Anneessens, on which you will encounter a memorial to the freedom fighter Frans Anneessens (1660–1719), who was executed by the Austrians in 1719.

82__The Pigeon Memorial
Secret messages in World War I

Announcement by German army command from 16 November, 1914: 'The owners of pigeons and pigeon lofts of any kind are to register them ... An evacuation of pigeons out of the city is forbidden'. The Germans had long suspected that there was regular hostile communication by carrier pigeon inside Belgium, with important dispatches about the condition of the German armed forces. Then they managed 'to shoot down a pigeon on the way to the enemy'. Announcement from 3 May, 1915: 'Any pigeons in the territory of the 4th army are to be killed before 8 o'clock in the evening (German time), on 6 May of this year. Any transportation of live pigeons is forbidden'. With this came the threat of severe punishment. And the first sentences. Announcement from 22 February, 1916: 'By court-martial ruling, in terms of the directive of the commander-in-chief of the 4th army, the Belgians (several names) are each sentenced to two years' imprisonment for the illegal ownership of pigeons'.

The memorial for the soldier pigeons of World War I was unveiled in March 1931. It depicted a beautiful antique goddess, who symbolises the fatherland. From her outstretched right hand she releases a pigeon into the air on a secret mission, while in the other she holds a palm branch, thus commemorating the Belgian pigeons who 'fell' for the fatherland. At the same time, encircled by garlands of leaves and laurel and the numbers 1914 and 1918, a homage to the pigeon breeders who placed their animals at the army's disposal and who lost them in the war for the fatherland is emblazoned on the memorial in golden letters.

The memorial with its spacious entranceway to the bronze statue, which stands on a granite pedestal, was designed by the architect Georges Hano, who was also responsible for the Brussels Parliament. The statue was realised by the Brussels sculptor Victor Voets.

Address Rue Locquenghin between Quai aux Barques and Quai à la Houille, 1000 Brussels | Getting there Metro 1 or 5 to Sainte-Catherine/Sint-Katelijne | Hours Accessible 24 hours | Tip Directly opposite is the memorial for the dead of the armoured units of both world wars. The Neo-Classical building of the Brussels Parliament at Rue du Lombard 69 with its superimposed assembly room is worth a look, as is the honeycombed building of the Parlement francophone bruxellois next door, dating from 2014.

83 __ The Pilgrimage Site

The Marian grotto – Lourdes in the middle of the city

You may believe you're experiencing an apparition, right in the middle of the mainly Muslim neighbourhood of Jette. Entering a small church through a gate on the left, you will come face to face with an impressive replica of the grotto at Lourdes. It is considered one of the most authentic of its kind.

Imitations of the Lourdes grotto were very much in fashion at the beginning of the 20th century, becoming popular local pilgrimage sites. 'Ave Maria' is emblazoned on the round arch above the marble altar at the entrance. It was a gift of King Albert I, who often visited the site.

The grotto behind the altar is covered with hundreds of devotional objects: written notes, pictures, crosses, candles, statues of the Virgin Mary, cuddly toys and other things, some of them very personal. On the right-hand side, enthroned in a recess in the rock and surrounded by golden roses, a copy of the Madonna, who apparently appeared to 14-year-old Bernadette Soubirous in the grotto at Lourdes in 1858. The sculptor Joseph-Hugues Fabisch (1812–1886) modelled the Marian figure for Lourdes in 1864, according to the girl's statements. Underneath the Brussels version, Saint Bernadette prays on an original stone from Lourdes, embedded in a marble slab.

Pilgrimages to Lourdes are made to heal and alleviate illness or to request people be delivered from danger or returned safely from war. That's how it was with the small church 'Our Lady of Lourdes', built in 1913 and the Jette grotto, consecrated two years later, on 15 August, 1915, in the middle of World War I, with over 20,000 people in attendance. In the meantime, Jette has become 'Lourdes of the north'. A small adjacent park with a dense stock of trees is conducive to contemplation. The foot of a six-metre-high cross with a statue of Jesus marks the start of a 'way of the cross' route with numerous coloured altars.

Address Rue Léopold I 296, 1090 Brussels (Jette) | Getting there Tram 51 to Woeste or bus 49 or 88 to Woeste or Loyauté | Hours Daily 9am–4pm, Sun 9am–5pm | Tip The small Parc Baudouin in the north of Jette with the former monastery Sacré-Cœur de Jette is a very appealing and quiet space (Avenue du Sacré-Cœur 8).

84_ The Pilot
Air raid on the Gestapo headquarters

It's early in the morning of Wednesday 20 January, 1943. A squadron of British Royal Air Force fighter-bombers is on the way home after attacking enemy positions near Ghent. On the outskirts of Brussels, a pilot suddenly pulls his Hawker Typhoon out of formation and flies towards the city centre, without orders to this effect, completely off his own bat. He flies low over the Boitsfort racecourse and then along the wide Avenue Franklin Roosevelt and into Avenue Louise. The target: the notorious Gestapo headquarters at Louise 453, a 12-storey high-rise building seized by the Nazis. This is where the Germans had run their regime of terror for months, where people detained arbitrarily are tortured in the cellar. The father of the young pilot had also been murdered by the Nazis. He attacks the building in a nosedive, wrenching the plane upwards just before the façade. He fires into the various floors with his aircraft cannon, covering the building with grenades and bullets. Numerous members of the SS are killed or injured. House 453 is in flames. Many citizens of Brussels come together and rejoice at this unexpected attack on the headquarters of the hated Gestapo. In the meantime, the pilot is on his way back to his unit in England.

The pilot was 31-year-old, Brussels-born Jean Michel de Selys Longchamps, a member of a Belgian aristocratic family. The young baron, in exile in Britain, belonged to No. 609 Squadron of the Royal Air Force. Seven months after his heroic operation in Avenue Louise, he crashed during landing after being hit in a dogfight over Ostend.

On the bullet-riddled building, which is still standing today, a memorial plaque pays tribute to the young lieutenant's heroic act. A gilded bust of the pilot, designed by Belgian sculptor Paul Boedts, has stood on the central reservation of Avenue Louise, in front of number 453, since 1993.

BARON
Jean de SELYS
LONGCHAMPS

Address Avenue Louise 453, 1000 Brussels | **Getting there** Tram 93 or 94 to Abbaye and Legrand | **Hours** Accessible 24 hours | **Tip** It is worthwhile taking a look at the Abbaye de la Cambre, founded in 1201, and the gracefully laid out gardens of the former Cistercian monastery.

CAPITAINE

85_The Piper

Peter Pan and Parc d'Egmont

The shortest route from Sablon to the elegant shopping streets on Place Louise leads through Parc d'Egmont. Fortunately, not many people know this and so the beautiful park of around 1.5 hectares remains a public yet discreet secret. Surrounded on all four sides by buildings, it is an oasis of peace right next to the city's fashionable but loud shopping centre.

The Passage Marguerite Yourcenar begins in Rue aux Laines/ Wolstraat. The path leads past reliefs with quotations from her novels – in remembrance of the author who is little known outside the francophone countries and who was the first woman to be admitted to the Académie française in 1980 (and whose birthplace is very close by) – and up a few steps into the park. Just to the right in the shade of an oak tree, Peter Pan is blowing his pipe. The bronze statue is usually besieged by children – there is after all lots to discover: rabbits, a squirrel, mice and the Lost Boys. The statue is a licensed copy of the original from London's Kensington Park, a present as a symbol of the friendship between British and Belgian children after World War I. The original was created by the British sculptor Sir George Frampton (1860–1928) in 1912.

The northern part of the park is bordered by Egmont or Arenberg Palace, which is best viewed from inside the park, even though the name 'Wild Boar Lawn' may suggest otherwise. The first building was commissioned in 1532 by Françoise van Luxemburg, widow of the Count of Egmont. The palace there today was built from 1752 on. After being destroyed several times, it now belongs to the Belgian state and serves for the reception of guests of state and for international conferences.

In the southeast corner of the park is an octagonal Gothic building, which is called Groote Pollepel, big cooking spoon, in the vernacular. It is in fact a well shaft from the 15th century.

Address Parc d'Egmont, Rue du Grand Cerf or Boulevard de Waterloo 31 (Passage de Milan) and 33 (next to Hilton), Rue aux Laines/Wolstraat (Passage Marguerite Yourcenar), 1000 Brussels | Getting there Metro 2 or 6 or tram 92 or 93 to Louise/Louiza or Petit Sablon | Hours Daily 8am–8pm | Tip The estate's former orangery is now called La Fabrique en Ville and is a restaurant with a beautiful patio.

86__ The Pissoir
Sainte-Catherine's special service

It would be completely unthinkable in most places: officially being allowed to urinate on a church, organised wild-peeing so to speak. Not so in Brussels, at the venerable Eglise Sainte-Catherine – diagonally opposite the Quai aux Briques, a stone's throw from the Fish Market. The urinal was installed here officially as a special service to the many beer drinkers of the city.

Covered in graffiti, it 'decorates' the exterior façade of the church, built from 1854 – screens allow for discreet execution, but cannot belie the 'special' flair of a public toilet. If you intend to quickly do your business in the toilets of one of the chic fish restaurants without having sat at a table first, the serving staff will politely, but bluntly, point you to the church wall. No one knows who was ultimately responsible for the urinal on Saint Catherine's church. The thing is just there.

Perhaps the pissoir was only able to establish itself in this privileged place because the church, built on the old harbour basin, has never really been much liked by the locals. It is a 'child' of the unpopular architect Joseph Poelaert (1817–1879), who had also built the monstrous Palace of Justice on behalf of Leopold II. The fact that the church, which had replaced a previous 15th-century building, was 'tinkered with' for over two decades through a lack of money, to ultimately end in a mix of Romanesque, Gothic and Renaissance styles, did the rest.

Because of the use of cheap building materials, the triple-naved church was already seen as in danger of collapse in the 1930s, and in the 1960s the authorities even considered razing it completely due to a need for parking spaces. Today Sainte-Catherine, as well as the atmospheric Place Sainte-Catherine with its fishmongers and pleasant outdoor eating, is a fixed part of the cityscape. Just like the pissoir on its façade.

Address Sainte-Catherine, Place Sainte-Catherine/Sint-Katelijneplein, 1000 Brussels | Getting there Metro 1 or 5 to Sainte-Catherine/Sint-Katelijne | Hours Accessible 24 hours | Tip The Tour Noir, the Black Tower, in between two new buildings on Place Sainte-Catherine, is a remnant of the first Brussels city wall from the 13th century.

87_ The Plaque

A global star from Ixelles/Elsene

There are those from Brussels whose names everyone associates with the city. Maurice Béjart for example, Eddy Merckx and of course Jacques Brel. There are others, however, that few know about. One of them is the fashion designer Ira von Fürstenberg and another is Audrey Hepburn. The actress, star of films such as *Breakfast at Tiffany's* and *War and Peace*, won all four of the important prizes awarded by the American entertainment industry – Oscar, Emmy, Grammy and Tony – but she wasn't actually American herself.

Audrey Kathleen Ruston was born the daughter of the English banker Joseph Victor Anthony Ruston and his Dutch wife Ella, Baroness van Heemstra in 1929 at Rue Keyenveld 48 in the Brussels neighbourhood of Ixelles/Elsene – her father later changed her name to Hepburn-Ruston. At the age of six weeks, the baby fell ill with whooping cough and almost died of asphyxiation. Audrey lived in Brussels for six years, a childhood about which very little is known. Subsequently she attended a girls' school in Kent. Her parents divorced and she moved to live near Arnhem with her mother and her two half brothers in 1939. The family survived the war and German occupation, Audrey Hepburn under the name Edda van Heemstra. A first career as a ballet dancer failed. Her muscles were too weak as a result of wartime malnutrition. She worked as a model and acted in two small films. The author Colette (1873–1954) discovered her for a Broadway production. Hollywood then became aware of the young woman and she received an Oscar for her very first lead role in *Roman Holiday*. Audrey Hepburn became an international star.

At Rue Keyenveld 48, a simple brass plaque commemorates Audrey Hepburn, who said of herself: 'My biography probably should have read: I was born in Brussels, Belgium on 4 May, 1929 … and died six weeks later.' Fortunately she didn't – Audrey Hepburn died in 1993.

CERCLE D'HISTOIRE LOCALE D'IXELLES

ICI
NAQUIT
LE 4 MAI 1929
LA COMEDIENNE

AUDREY HEPBURN

Address Rue Keyenveld/Keienveldstraat 48, 1050 Brussels (Ixelles/Elsene) | Getting there Tram 92, 93 or 94 to Stephanie or bus 54 or 71 to Quartier St Boniface | Hours Accessible 24 hours | Tip A bust of the Argentinian author Julio Cortàzar, who was born the son of a diplomat in Brussels, can be found on Avenue Louis Lepoutre (Place Brugmann). The bust and a plaque on the corner house (to the right) commemorate him.

88 — The Razor Shop

A purveyor of knives and scissors to the royal court

It won't be long until the A. Jamart building – the name of the original founder still adorns the shop to this day – is 200 years old. Au Grand Rasoir was established in 1821 and then quickly grew into three operations with its own knife production facility. Black Thursday, the crash on the New York stock exchange on 24 October, 1929, ruined the Jamart family and the company went bust. The Cielen family took over the original shop and continued the business of selling knives there in almost unaltered décor, now already in their third generation. The current owner, Jean Cielen, who drove with his grandfather to Solingen as a young boy to buy blades, is in his mid-60s and starting to think about handing over the management of the shop to his daughter Anne. Having learned from her father, she too has stayed true to the family tradition and is a specialist in blades of all kinds.

The shop for all manner of bladed instruments is located right next to Brussels city council: knives and scissors, from robust Opinels for eight euros to hand-forged Damascene blades for several thousand euros. There are knives from France and Japan on sale, knives from Solingen too of course; penknives for everyday use and knives for professionals, whether chefs or butchers; scissors for tailors and household use. Around 60 artisanal manufacturers supply the shop with close to 2,000 different knives.

Jean Cielen feels especially indebted to the 'great razor' in the company name. Father and daughter recognise joyfully that well-groomed beards are back in fashion and with them the associated utensils: good blades, whetstones, badger-hair shaving brushes and similar accessories. 'Young people are concerned with quality again', they both agree. And that is what a purveyor to the royal court offers – the business also continues to officially carry this title in its name.

Address Au Grand Rasoir, Rue de l'Hôpital / Gasthuisstraat 7, 1000 Brussels, +32 (0)2 5124962, www.coutellerie-jamart.be | **Getting there** Metro 1 or 5 to Gare Centrale / Centraal Station or bus 48 or 95 to Parlement Bruxellois | **Hours** Mon – Fri 9am – 6.30pm, Sat 9am – 6pm | **Tip** There are many special shops that are dedicated to just one thing in Brussels. Opposite the razor shop, at Rue Saint-Jean 47, Music Shop stocks anything to do with the electric guitar, whereas Azzato, Rue de la Violette 42 sells instruments from lutes to bagpipes.

89 __ Résistance

The museum of Belgian resistance

That the museum documenting Belgian resistance against the country's occupation by the Germans between 1940 and 1945 and the ever-present terror of the Nazis is housed in an old residential house out in Anderlecht, has a historical reason and is itself part of the story of Belgian résistance. There was a printing plant in Rue van Lint, and this is where the 'Faux Soir' was produced and printed on 9 November, 1943 during the German occupation. It was a fake, perfect imitation underground edition of the daily paper *Le Soir* (*The Evening*). Editors of the official paper collaborated with the German occupying forces. This rebellious counter-edition, however, openly called for resistance. The printing plates of the original edition are on display in the museum and the story of the counterfeit and its initiator Ferdinand Wellens is told.

This museum, small, yet documenting such an important part of Belgian history, was opened in 1972, but is to this day widely unknown, even in Brussels. The project, run by two employees and financed to a large extent by a 600-member sponsoring association, receives around 2,000 visitors a year – mainly academics, school classes and veterans – far too few for this very honourable part of Belgian history. The Belgians should continue to be proud of the resistance with which they opposed the Nazis. In no other occupied country were more Jews saved from the grasp of the Nazis and their machinery of destruction by civilians or completely normal citizens and partisans than in Belgium from 1941 on. Thousands of Jews were hidden, sometimes for many years, in Belgian families at the risk of their own lives.

The museum traces Belgian resistance by means of many original documents. In includes the archive of the 'Front de l'Indépendance' and other organisations and has a library dedicated to resistance texts.

Address Musée de la Résistance de Belgique, Rue van Lint 14, 1070 Brussels (Anderlecht), +32 (0)2 5224041, www.museumresistance.be | **Getting there** Metro 2 or 6 to Clemenceau, tram 81 to Conseil or bus 46 to Albert I | **Hours** Mon–Fri 9am–noon & 1–4pm | **Tip** From the museum it is only a few metres along Rue van Lint to Anderlecht town hall, built between 1877 and 1879 by the Belgian architect Jules-Jacques Van Ysendyck (1836–1901) in a Neo-Flemish Renaissance style.

90__The Retables

The perfection of Brabant school sculpture

In room 57 on the first floor of the grand Cinquantenaire Museum of art and history, which opened with 140 rooms in 1922, awaits a collection of offbeat altar art, which, despite the museum's many other highlights, you definitely shouldn't miss. The altarpieces and wooden retables from the Brabant school of sculpture from the end of the 15th century are some of the most important of their kind in the world.

In the centre of the wooden altarpieces from the workshops of Brussels, Antwerp and Mechelen, which were some of the most important centres of production of precious retables in the Middle Ages, there is generally a crucifixion group or the coronation of the Virgin Mary, with numerous realistic and detail-rich figures. The painted and gilded carvings tell biblical stories in the colourful costumes of the times in the most limited of spaces, so that they seem like theatre pieces. Brussels was one of the most important centres of production at the end of the 15th century, before woodcarving in Antwerp became ever more important at the beginning of the 16th century. Among the late-Gothic Brussels retables, those of Saint George by the sculptor Jan Borremans from 1493 and the retable of the Passion by an unknown artist from around 1470 are particularly noteworthy. In terms of the altar pictures from the Antwerp School, the Passion by Oplinter from 1530 stands out. In total, there are 15 complete retables on show in the Musées Royaux d'Art et d'Histoire, most of them commissioned by wealthy benefactors.

The high-quality carved altar pictures required the close collaboration of various craftsmen: carpenters and joiners for the framing, sculptors and woodcarvers for the filigree statuettes, gilders and painters for the visual appearance. Individual craftsmen often liked to immortalise their workshops with marks and initials on the altar pictures.

Address Musée du Cinquantenaire/Jubelparkmuseum, Parc du Cinquantenaire/Jubelpark 10, 1000 Brussels, +32 (0)2 7417331, www.kmkg-mrah.be | Getting there Metro 1 or 5 to Merode or Schuman, tram 81 to Merode, or bus 22, 27 or 80 to Gallier; car park at the museum | Hours Tue–Fri 9.30am–5pm, Sat & Sun 10am–5pm | Tip The museum is home to a huge variety of European and non-European cultural treasures. The collection of historic horse-drawn carriages, including the wedding carriages of Leopold I and Napoleon III, is highly recommended.

91_Rue Dansaert

Fashionable, chic, quirky and expensive

Rue Dansaert, a stone's throw away from Bourse, has a chequered history. First a financial centre, then a lacklustre shopping street and a rather run-down drag in the 1980s and 1990s. But today it has found its way back to former glories. The street is chic and popular among young people – often Flemish speaking and well funded. This is largely down to fashion. Three-dozen boutiques, one after another on a 400-metre stretch, and none of them chain stores.

Antwerp had previously been considered Belgium's centre of fashion. The young guns of the 'Antwerp six', with the designers Dries van Noten and Ann Demeulemeester, shook up the international fashion scene good and proper. Then came Rue Dansaert in Brussels. Because the quarter in the middle of the city centre was on the decline, many large apartments and studios were available on the cheap. And it was precisely this that attracted young creatives. They could try out new ideas without too much financial risk. Elvis Pompilio, eccentric hatter to the royal family, Johanne Riss, Olivier Strelli, Annemie Verbeke – they all presented their first designs on Rue Dansaert: sustainable, unconventional and avant-garde fashion. Because the EU employs thousands of young people, there were also customers with an interest in fashion and the money needed to buy it.

Many of the designers have become very well known in the meantime and of course the prices of their clothes have risen too. The same goes for everything else in the area, especially accommodation. Today, the area around Dansaert is chic and sparkles with a new lustre – superb for visitors, but expensive for residents. There is certainly plenty of fashion to choose from and it's fun walking from one to the next, looking and perhaps even buying something. The whole development began in 1984 with Sonja Noels' clothes shop Stijl, still at number 74.

Address Rue Dansaert, 1000 Brussels | Getting there Tram 3, 4 or 32 or bus 86, 126 or 127 to Bourse/Beurs | Hours Accessible 24 hours | Tip The clearance sales in Brussels are worthwhile, whether advertised as soldes or uitverkoop. The norm is 30 to 70 per cent discount, especially for clothes.

92__The Senne
The river no one sees and no one knows

All great cities are located on rivers: Paris, Rome and London. Only Brussels isn't. At least that's the way it looks, but that isn't in fact the truth. Brussels is located on a river, the Senne. It's already suggested by the name Brussels, which means 'place by the marsh'. Admittedly, the Senne is a small river, only 103 kilometres long, fed by the Maelbeek and the Woluwe, and an indirect tributary of the Scheldt via the Dijle and Rupel. In fact, it was actually called the Braine until the 10th century. Charles of Lower Lorraine, from western France, took up residence on a fortified island in the wetlands of the Braine and introduced the name Senne in reference to the Seine.

There were once tanneries, paper mills and breweries on the Senne. They used its water and fed the waste water straight back into it. The Senne was practically an open drainage channel, stank to high heaven and was quite rightly thought of as one of the most polluted rivers in Europe. That is why it was completely covered over during the restructuring of the city centre in 1867. And so today there's nowhere in Brussels where the Senne can be seen – well, almost nowhere. Only a small opening next to Place Saint-Gery offers a view of the river.

In Rue de la Grande Île is an old 17th-century postal station, a two-storey red brick building, the Lion d'Or, golden lion. The whole complex of buildings was repaired in 1980. In the process two beautiful courtyards opened up on both sides of the former brewery and bakery buildings of the adjoining monastery of Riches-Claires. This building bridged the Senne, which was then exposed again. The riverbed is reconstructed across a few metres, an unfamiliar sight even for locals.

The Senne is certainly visible outside the city. The iris, which adorns the coat of arms of the Brussels Capital Region, thrives in the wetland areas along the river.

Address Rue de la Grande Île/Groot-Eilandstraat 1, 1000 Brussels | **Getting there** Metro 3 or 4, tram 32 or bus 86 to Bourse/Beurs | **Hours** The courtyard of the Lion d'Or is private. The barred gate is open and the courtyard accessible during the day. As long as the tranquillity of the place is respected, a visit won't bother anyone. | **Tip** The church of the Riches-Claires monastery is worth a visit. It was built by Lucas Faydherbe, a pupil of Rubens. The slate-roofed wooden spire and the white marble altar are particularly beautiful.

93 The Shoah Memorial
Pausing for reflection in 'Maghreb' Anderlecht

Belgium's response seemed very late when, on 19 April, 1970, as part of the celebrations marking the 25th anniversary of victory and the liberation of the concentration camps, a memorial for the Jews deported and murdered during German occupation was inaugurated. Until that point, Belgian historiography and the public realm had, to a large extent, suppressed the persecution of the Jews, despite the fact that many Jewish compatriots had been saved by a courageous civilian population, especially in Belgium. In the years after the end of the war, Walloons and Flemings were occupied first and foremost with mutual recriminations, accusing each other of having collaborated with the Nazis after the occupation in May 1940. The role played by the resistance couldn't be agreed for a long time.

The memorial was designed by two Belgian architects, André Godart and Odon Dupire, and broadly follows the brief laid out for the state-initiated national memorial for Belgium's 'Jewish martyrs'. A crypt is enclosed by a star-shaped structure, mostly in concrete and steel, which can also function as an open-air synagogue. The names of all 24,000-plus Belgian Jews murdered are immortalised on black granite plates sunk into the concrete walls alongside an urn containing ashes from Auschwitz. An additional monument, erected in 1979, expressly commemorates the 'Jewish heroes' who were killed as Belgian resistance fighters.

From the beginning, the memorial in Anderlecht, a district in which many Jews once lived but now inhabited predominately by Maghreb Muslims, had to be protected and guarded. It was trespassed, graffitied and vandalised time and again, reaching an inglorious climax in the summer of 2006 with the destruction of the crypt and the theft of the urn. The whole complex was then radically rebuilt and since then only opens sporadically by special arrangement.

Address Monument National aux Martyrs Juifs de Belgique à Bruxelles, Place des Martyrs Juifs, Rue Emile Carpentier, 1070 Brussels (Anderlecht) | Getting there Bus 116, 117, 118, 136, 137, 140, 141, 142, 144, 145, 170 or 171 to Anderlecht Grondel | Hours By arrangement: Musée de la Résistance de Belgique, Rue van Lint 14, organises guided tours (+32 (0)2 5224041) | Tip You can find out a lot more about Jewish life in Brussels in the Jewish Museum (Musée Juif de Belgique, Rue des Minimes/Miniemenstraat 21).

94_ The Silver Spheres

The molecule of iron magnified 165 billion times

The promise of a bright future: the Atomium. It became the emblem of the 1958 World's Fair and a symbol for supposedly safe and clean nuclear power. The Federal Republic of Germany rented one of the spheres, where the nuclear chemistry pioneer Otto Hahn welcomed international guests. The bold structure – a steel skeleton with aluminium skin – was supposed to stand on the grounds of the fair for exactly half a year, before being torn down. At least that was the plan.

André Waterkeyn (1917–2005), engineer and director of the Belgian steel manufacturer Fabrimetal, designed the structure. It was built by the Belgian architect brothers André (1914–1988) and Jean Polak (1920–2012) in only 2 years – 9 spheres, each with a diameter of 18 metres, 6 of them accessible, connected by 20 tubes with a diameter of 3.30 metres and 29 metres long, 102 metres tall and around 2,400 tonnes in weight. A mighty colossus, that at the same time seems so light, almost delicate. Tourists love the photo opportunity that makes it look like they are holding the atom in the palm of their hand. But few tourists actually go inside the Atomium. Not only do they miss the ingenious light design by Ingo Maurer, but also the ride on the 35-metre escalator, the longest in Europe at the time, through the illuminated tubes between individual spheres. In fact, all of the staircases are delicate works of art. A visit to the restaurant in the uppermost sphere, with a fascinating panoramic view, is also highly recommended.

The Atomium was given a general overhaul between 2003 and 2006. After all, the 'temporary arrangement' had been standing for 45 years by that point. It is now 100 tonnes heavier, as the new outer skin of the spheres is made of stainless-steel sheeting. The skin is studded with thousands of lights, invisible during the day, but revealing a very special effect at night.

Address Square de l'Atomium, 1020 Brussels (Laeken / Laken), +32 (0)2 4754775 | Getting there Metro 6, tram 7 or bus 84 or 88 to Heysel / Heizel | Hours Daily 10am – 6pm | Tip The ring road around the city centre was built for the World's Fair in 1958, mostly six lanes above ground and four lanes underground: two floors against gridlock.

95__The Slaughterhouse
Shopping in the abattoirs of Anderlecht

The halls of the old Anderlecht slaughterhouse are only a short walk away from Midi. During the week, the slaughterhouse operates as you'd expect, processing 230,000 animals a year. But from Friday to Sunday the halls transform into the second biggest weekly market in Brussels.

And what a market it is! Once you pass the two life-size bronze bulls at the entrance, you'll find yourself slap bang in the middle of a lively scene. You can find literally anything for sale here, and at the best prices in the city. There's a section for household goods and one for (cheap) clothes. There are electronic devices (new, used and 'fell off the back of a lorry') and children's toys. All around the grounds, cars and smuggled cigarettes are traded.

There are three areas that are particularly special: first the flea market, brocante. Here you'll find it all, from bric-à-brac and knick-knacks via second-hand goods to real antiques. Not always what you happen to be looking for, but interesting and exciting things nonetheless. Then there's 'Food-Met'. Anderlecht is, even by Brussels' standards, especially multicultural. With people from over 180 countries living here, the demand for specific foods from central Africa, the Maghreb or Indochina is high. Accordingly, you will find varieties of fruit and vegetables that most northern Europeans rarely get to see alongside the peas, carrots and beans. And then – no surprise considering the location – there's the fresh meat (including offal, pigs' feet and sheep heads), poultry (quails, pigeons, guinea fowl and partridges), game, in season, and – also obvious in a country by the sea – fresh fish and seafood. Apropos fresh: live animals are sold in the third section – hares, ducks and chickens, sometimes also songbirds. Around 30,000 people visit the abattoir at the weekend. Those scared off from visiting the reputed no-go areas really do miss out.

Address Rue Ropsy Chaudron 24, 1070 Brussels (Anderlecht), +32 (0)2 5215419, www.abattoir.be | Getting there Metro 2 or 6 or bus 46 to Clemenceau | Hours Fri–Sun 7am–2pm | Tip Brasserie La Paix 1892, opposite the market entrance, was once a pub with hearty food for market suppliers. However, the new chef David Martin has earned himself a star with some fantastic cooking.

96__ The Solvay Library

In the footprints of the great industrialist and patron

The building is a masterpiece of 20th-century eclecticism, a mix of various architectural styles, in particular numerous elements of Art Nouveau.

It was built on behalf of, and named after, the chemist, business-man and patron Ernest Solvay (1838–1922) in 1902 to the blue-prints of the architects Constant Bosmans (1851–1936) and Henri Vandeveld (1851–1929; no relation to Henry Van de Velde). Its location on a hill in Leopold Park, designed in the style of an English garden, means it is not far from today's EU Parliament. Endowed and financed as a centre for science and ultimately a sociological institute of the University of Brussels, the faculty in Leopold Park lost its function in 1967 due to a lack of space, but was still used as a branch of the library for a long time, before it closed completely in 1981, stood empty for more than 10 years and was in grave danger of falling into complete disrepair. The building was completely renovated in the 1990s and finally reopened with a new lustre in 1994.

The centrepiece and all-dominating room is the library, which is like a church nave in its size and impact. The universally Art Nouveau interior – significantly inspired by the sociologist Emile Waxweiler (1867–1916), once director of the Solvay-Institute for Sociology – with its innovative teaching and study spaces tailored to individual learning, is captivating: the painted panelled ceiling, the ornate mahogany wood panelling, the floor mosaics and the elaborate glass paintings. The large red reading room, with its numerous golden decorations, is lined over two floors and galleries, with wrought-iron railings, by row upon row of mahogany shelves full of historic books. But none of them can be borrowed. After its five million euro restoration, the Solvay library is now a location for events, concerts, exhibitions, conferences and receptions.

Address Parc Léopold, Rue Belliard 137, 1040 Brussels, +32 (0)2 7387596, www.edi cio.be/fr/bibliotheque-solvay | **Getting there** Metro 1 or 5 to Maelbeek or Schuman or bus 27 to Parc Léopold | **Hours** Can be viewed from the outside. Interior viewing only possible on guided tours by Arkadia (Rue Royale 2–4, 1000 Brussels, +32 (0)2 5636153, www.arkadia.be) | **Tip** Parc Tournay-Solvay (Chaussée de la Hulpe), laid out around 1900 with a splendid rose garden and a once grandiose villa, today a vacant ruin, is well worth visiting.

97__The Square

Conferring inside the Kunstberg

The spectacular glass building is especially captivating when night falls and it is visible from far and wide, illuminated in blue and sitting on the Kunstberg like an angular gemstone.

The three-storey, 16-metre-high glass cube stands above the main entrance of the new congress centre, which is sunk into the ground. This opened in 2009 after a planning and building phase of seven years, finally taking the place of the former Palais des Congrès, built in 1958 in the course of the World's Fair.

Now it has been fundamentally renewed and its capacity more than doubled. A second entrance into the cube can be reached via a terrace higher up. The glass structure of the cube, which looks like the bifurcation of a tree, transparent and bathed in light, with visible escalators and gangways, corresponds with the garden landscaping of the architect René Pechère (1908 – 2002). The cube is the flagship of the 52,000-square-metre cultural forum and claims to visually transport Mont des Arts into modernity, as the central entrance area, in a similar way to the glass pyramid of the Paris Louvre.

The 70-million-euro project Square was developed and realised by the prominent Brussels architecture office A.2R.C, founded in 1983, taking into account the structure of the old Palais des Congrès. There are 27 conference rooms of differing size across 13,000 subterranean square metres. On top of that, there are 3,700 square metres of exhibition space for receptions, fashion shows and events of all kinds, spacious foyers, a restaurant, the brasserie with a terrace and a ballroom with a view over Brussels. Many of the multifunctional halls and rooms, each designed in a uniform colour, have natural light. In the foyer, you will also find completely refurbished and restored monumental murals by Paul Delvaux, René Magritte and Louis van Lint from the 1960s – utterly captivating.

Address Square Brussels Meeting Centre, Rue du Musée/Museumstraat 8, 1000 Brussels, +32 (0)2 5151300, www.squarebrussels.com | Getting there Metro 1 or 5 to Gare Centrale/ Centraal Station and Parc/Park or bus 38 or 71 to Royale | Hours Accessible 24 hours from the outside | Tip A few steps up the hill (Rue du Musée 8) you will come across the six-metre-high, *Whirling Ear* mobile by the American sculptor Alexander Calder (1898–1976) from 1958, installed in a pond.

98 __ The Statues
The guilds and the resistance against Spain

The Place du Petit Sablon across from the late-Gothic church Notre-Dame de Sablon is tranquil, a carefully cultivated oasis of green with clipped hedges, flower beds and benches to rest your feet. But before you sit down, do a circuit of the trapezoidal park, created in 1890, which is enclosed with an ornately designed wrought-iron fence, and take a journey back in time to the 16th century, into the world of Brussels' trade and craftsmen's guilds. On 48 Gothic pillars, bronze representatives of their time greet passersby, each equipped with the corresponding props of their trade: the upholsterer with a reel of cotton, coppersmith with a hammer, the fat seller with a slaughtered goose or the armourer with a sword. All of the figures are thoroughly composed in every detail. The architect of Place du Petit Sablon, the Belgian Hendrik Beyaert (1823–1894), assigned the creation of the figures to the painter Xavier Mellery (1845–1921) and the Art Nouveau architect Paul Hankar (1859–1901), who worked in Beyaert's office from 1879 to 1892 and was later to become one of the greats of his genre. As a reminder of their boss, they gave some of the modelled craftsmen Beyaert's facial features.

The rear section of the gently climbing garden, which served as a cemetery for a nearby hospital from the 13th to the 18th century, is dominated by the Counts of Egmont and Horne on a plinth in the middle of a sparkling fountain, who led the insurgency against Spanish rule under Philip II and were beheaded in 1568 on the Grand-Place. The memorial, made in 1864 by sculptor Charles Auguste Fraikin (1817–1893), shows the two freedom fighters on their way to the scaffold and originally stood in front of the Maison du Roi, the place of their execution. The fountain is surrounded by a semicircle of 10 statues, which represent politicians, intellectuals and artists of the 16th century.

Address Place du Petit Sablon / Kleine Zavel, Rue de la Régence / Regentschapsstraat, 1000 Brussels | Getting there Metro 3 or 6 to Louise / Louiza or Porte de Namur / Naamsepoort or tram 92 or 93 or bus 27 or 95 to Petit Sablon | Hours Accessible 24 hours | Tip Not far from the park is a synagogue from 1875 (Rue de la Régence 32).

99__The Surrealist House

Magritte's motifs at every turn

In July 1930, René Magritte and his wife Georgette Berger came back to Brussels after a three-year stay in Paris and rented an unspectacular house in Rue Esseghem in the suburb of Jette. The married couple were to live here for 24 years.

A normal, three-storey, lower-middle-class house without luxury and without a huge studio became the centre of Belgian Surrealism. The Magrittes and their surrealist friends met here once a week, planned happenings or drafted treatises on questions of art or politics.

More than half of all of Magritte's famous pictures were created in this very house. And that's what makes it so appealing to visitors. Many elements or even models of the paintings are from here: you may recognise the glass doors of the parlour, the staircase, the fireplace, the 'guillotine' windows, yes, even the street lights in front of the property. Magritte wanted to unsettle habitual patterns of thinking and seeing by painting objects naturalistically, in order to then make them alien through unexpected combinations. He said of one of his most famous works, *The Treachery of Images* (*This is Not a Pipe*), 'One mustn't mistake a picture for an object that one can touch. And yet, could you stuff my pipe? No, it's just a representation, is it not? So if I had written on my picture, "This is a pipe", I'd have been lying. A representation of a jam sandwich is certainly not something that can be eaten.'

The lower floors of the house are faithfully furnished in its original style, with photos, manuscripts, letters and drawings. From the third floor you can see 'Studio Dongo' in the garden. Here Magritte marketed his 'commercial graphics', designed posters for theatre and music events and also cigarette packaging. René Magritte painted in the kitchen his whole life – it was warmer there and he was closer to his wife. The easel still stands there today.

Address René Magritte-Museum, Rue Esseghem 135, 1090 Brussels (Jette), +32 (0)2 4282626 | **Getting there** Tram 19, 51, 62 or 93 to Cimetière de Jette or bus 49, 53 or 88 to Woeste | **Hours** Wed–Sun 10am–6pm | **Tip** The Magritte Museum opened on Place Royale / Königsplatz in Brussels city centre in 2009 as part of the Royal Museums of Fine Arts. René Magritte and Georgette Berger are buried in Schaerbeek cemetery.

100__ The Swallow's-Nest Organ

A masterpiece by the organ builder Gerhard Grenzing

A very special musical treat has awaited visitors to Saint-Michel-et-Gudule, the Catholic Brussels cathedral and seat of the archbishop of Mechelen-Brussels, since the year 2000. That was when the swallow's-nest organ by renowned organ builder Gerhard Grenzing was fired up for the first time in the left front side of the main nave.

When in 1997 a call to tender for a new organ was made, the client let it be known that a work of art for the third century should be created, an organ with around 60 registers and four manuals. And all of this ingeniously integrated in the comparatively narrow (only 11-metre-wide) and delicate nave of the slender Gothic church, without damaging the statics of the architecture under the depth and the weight of the organ. The workshop of the German organ builder Gerhard Grenzing, near Barcelona, emerged as the winner of the competition. The plan: a tripartite organ, 17 metres in height. A swallow's-nest organ of such size had never before been built in Europe. The organ was completely installed in a gigantic hall in Spain, played and then disassembled again, transported to Brussels and finally hung with huge cranes at the height of the triforiums from 1273 in the nave of Saint-Michel. The organ was ceremoniously consecrated on 1 June, 2000, Ascension Day.

With this the cathedral, built in Gothic style on the Treurenberg between the lower and upper parts of the city, whose construction began in 1226 and was only completed with the two spires at the end of the 15th century, was given a top-drawer instrument. Since then the best local and international organists have given concerts on the swallow's-nest organ – embedded in the ambience of this church, flooded in light from 16 large windows with 1,200 glass paintings from the 16th century.

Address Saint-Michel-et-Gudule, Rue Place Sainte-Gudule, 1000 Brussels | **Getting there** Metro 1 or 5 to Gare Centrale/Centraal Station | **Hours** Mon–Fri 7am–6pm, Sat 8.30am–3.30pm, Sun 2–6pm (for organ concerts see event information at www.cathedralisbruxellensis.be) | **Tip** In the crypt, parts of the previous 8th-century Romanesque chapel can still be made out, some of the oldest traces of the city's history.

101__ The Swan

Karl Marx and the 'German Workers' Club'

'Workers of the world, unite!' This phrase, the contents of which was to shape world history, was written in Brussels. It was here, together with his friend and comrade Friedrich Engels, that Karl Marx formulated his radical critique of the bourgeois social and economic order of his time in the middle of the 19th century: *The Communist Manifesto*. The call for the international proletariat to engage in class struggle was to become one of the foundations of Marxism.

Brussels was a centre of international exile in this period. Numerous left-wing thinkers and politicians, who were ostracised or persecuted in their own countries, fled to the Belgian capital, much vaunted as cosmopolitan and liberal. Karl Marx also moved to Brussels in 1845, having been expelled from Paris. He lived and worked here for three years, until he was once again deported, living in Rue d'Ardenne in Ixelles from 1846 to 1848.

In 1847, Marx and Engels founded the 'German Workers' Educational Association' in Brussels. Le Cygne (The Swan) on the Grand-Place became the regular meeting place of the German socialists living in exile.

In this guild house – destroyed after the bombardment of Brussels city centre by the French in 1695, completely renovated in 1698 in new baroque glory, since 1720 the guild house of the butchers – debating and partying were given equal standing. *The Communist Manifesto*, published in the revolutionary year of 1848, was partly conceived and written here in 1847 as the programme for the recently formed Communists League. The Belgian Workers' Party was also founded in The Swan in 1885. A plaque on the house refers, however, rather to the 'social' side of things: 'Karl Marx celebrated New Year's Eve 1847/1848 in this house with the German Workers' Club and the Association Démocratique. He lived in Brussels from February 1845 to March 1848.'

Address Grand-Place / Grote Markt 9, 1000 Brussels | **Getting there** Metro 1 or 5 to Bourse / Beurs and Gare Centrale / Centraal Station | **Hours** Accessible 24 hours | **Tip** Today The Swan houses the restaurant La Maison du Cygne and is the base and headquarters of Cercle Ommegang, the organiser of the city celebration of the same name. The French author Victor Hugo lived in Le Pigeon (Grand-Place 26–27) from 1852 on.

102__The Terrace
Musical panoramic view

You can ride up to the sixth floor of the former department store Old England, a gem of Brussels-style Art Nouveau architecture built in the last two years of the 19th century, without actually visiting the museum. Here you will be tempted by the cafeteria and the museum restaurant, where members of the fine Brussels society once met for afternoon tea, as a rooftop terrace opens out and offers one of the most exclusive views of Brussels. Through the intricate wrought-iron grillwork, which entwines the corner turret set on the side and above the upper storeys of the richly ornate building, there are views out to the Town Hall on Grand-Place and to the Koekelberg with its massive Basilica. You can sit outside on summer days and can see out almost as far as the city limits from the sun deck at the rear part of the upper floor, which looks like a pergola from the outside with its central dome and the oversized arched windows.

The Old England, an architectural masterpiece of cast iron, steel and glass by the Belgian architect Paul Saintenoy (1862–1952), a contemporary of Victor Horta and Paul Hankar, is a preeminent example of Brussels Art Nouveau. After it closed its doors as an exclusive department store for Brussels high society, with international repute, it was, for a time, threatened with ruin.

Since 2000, the Old England has been home to MIM, the Brussels Musical Instrument Museum, one of the most important collections of its kind in the world with around 7,000 instruments. Around 1,200 exhibits are displayed over four floors – from the old Egyptian harp to 20th-century electronics. A focus: keyboard and stringed instruments. And you certainly shouldn't miss the presentation of instruments made by the Belgian Adolphe Sax (1814–1894), who studied at The Royal Conservatory of Brussels from 1835, became an instrument maker and invented the saxophone.

Address MIM, Rue Montagne de la Cour / Hofberg 2, 1000 Brussels, +32 (0)2 5450130, www.mim.be | Getting there Metro 1 or 5 or tram 92 or 94 to Gare Centrale / Centraal Station and Parc / Park | Hours Tue–Fri 9.30am–5pm, Sat & Sun 10am–5pm | Tip The architect Paul Saintenoy renovated the neighbouring Hotel Ravenstein (built in late Brabant Gothic style) in 1894 and realised the adjacent Pharmacie Delacre in 1898.

103 Théâtre Flamand

The Koninklijke Vlaamse Shouwburg on the old harbour

The Royal Flemish Theatre is located in Brussels' old harbour area. The streets right and left of the building border a former basin and a cattle market as an elongated rectangle and are called to this day 'Ashlar Quay' and 'Hay Quay'.

In 1779, the City of Brussels had a large building erected here as a warehouse and customs store. It was rededicated as an arsenal for the army in 1860 and converted into a theatre from 1883 by the architect Jean-Baptiste Baes (1848–1914). In accordance with its new use, the interior and exterior were completely renovated, the work being completed in 1887. In principle, Baes 'turned' the house 180 degrees. The old front elevation of the arsenal remained intact, but became the rear. Baes relocated the main entrance as part of a completely redesigned façade on Rue de Laeken. Art historians term the architectural style Eclecticism, a mixture of styles from various eras: a Gothic-like roof with Renaissance ornamentations and then balconies reinforced with forged iron railings running around four floors in an industrial architectural style. What sounds like a hotchpotch actually looks stately and is highly practical. The large balconies are not only pretty, they also serve as viewing platforms, break rooms and efficient emergency escape routes. When the theatre burned down almost completely in 1955, its multi-functionality was proven in a macabre way.

The building's exterior was restored after the fire, but inside, only the large stairs and the foyer with a bar on the first floor could be saved. But a visit is worthwhile for that alone. The auditorium and the theatre's technical facilities were brought up to date at the beginning of the century. Today, the programme is multicultural and cosmopolitan with performances in Dutch, French and other languages, often with surtitles. There are also exhibitions, concerts and dance performances.

Address Rue de Laeken / Lakensestraat 146, 1000 Brussels, +32 (0)2 2101112 | Getting there Metro 2 or 6, tram 5 or bus 47, 58 or 88 to Yser / IJzer | Hours An hour before the start of the respective event | Tip The nearby La Tentation (Temptation) is the place to go to eat and drink Spanish-Galician, but in particular to dance samba, bossa nova, salsa and swing, often to live music.

104__ The Tour & Taxis Hall
A new quarter and a music festival

You can see the imposing hall in the industrial architectural style of the early 20th century from the bumpy cobbled street right on the canal: 200 metres long, 60 metres wide, huge and majestic in brick and bluestone, decorated with towers. The Tour & Taxis building complex refers to the Belgian branch of the family who once governed the European postal service. The central building belongs to an extensive complex of halls on the 4,000-square-metre site.

When you enter the five-storey so-called Entrepot Royal through one of the portals on the two front sides, it will take your breath away: the central aisle is a hall as wide as a street, overarched by a glass roof more than 20 metres high; to the right and left are trendy shops, bars and cafés. All you can see of the four upper floors are the large, cast-iron galleries connected by bridges. Here lawyers, publishers, estate agents and even Disney Belgium have their offices. It's hard to believe that this building was a ruin 20 years previously.

In 1900, the Belgian railway developed the area on the canal for a new goods and logistics centre. At the start of the 1960s around 3,000 people worked here, but with the introduction of the European Customs Union in 1968, the building lost its function, stood vacant for many years and fell into disrepair. In 1990, the industrial wasteland was rediscovered for their purposes by the young generation: the empty halls and open spaces were the ideal place for a music festival.

Since then one of the most important festivals for world music takes place here for three days every year: the Couleur Café. All of the greats have played here: James Brown, Jimmy Cliff, Santana and Gilberto Gil. Now rich investors also recognised the potential of the site. Work began in 2001 and some of the results of a new, modern city quarter with an historical backdrop can already be seen.

Address Avenue du Port/Havenlaan 86c, 1000 Brussels, www.tour-taxis.com | Getting there Bus 14 or 15 to Tour et Taxis or bus 57 or 88 to Armateurs | Hours Daily 8am–midnight | Tip A new neighbourhood of ultra-modern glass high-rises is also emerging on Place Rogier. It would seem that Brussels is doing a New York.

105__The Town Hall

Art Deco in Forest/Vorst

Originally an independent, rural community to the south of Brussels, Forest/Vorst was discovered by rich townspeople in the middle of the 19th century. To begin with they built imposing villas in expansive parks, such as that of the ethnic German lace manufacturer Wilhelm Duden. Later they built factories, such as the Wielemans-Ceuppens brewery or the Lever soap factory. The community grew rapidly and had already reached 31,000 inhabitants by 1920. The administration department was bursting at the seams.

A new town hall was to provide the solution. The contract was given to the Belgian architect Jean-Baptiste Dewin (1873–1948) in 1925. Ten years later, after several quarrels about a suitable location, the foundations were laid, and in 1938 the town hall was finally officially inaugurated. It has been considered a masterpiece of Art Deco ever since. Strict geometric lines characterise the building, on the exterior yellow-red bricks, concrete and bluestone; inside marble, bluestone and brass.

Prominent artists were involved in its design. The gilded figures, which adorn the 50-metre tower in the style of a medieval belfry, are by Victor Rousseau, likewise the flat reliefs, which represent the most important local careers, including brewer and shoemaker. The glass windows were designed by Georges Balthus, the impressive interior with bluestone, brass and tropical wood from the Congo is by the De Coene brothers. Lamps, staircases, benches, desks and door fittings, all true to the style, are all completely preserved. The building and all of the furnishings have been listed since 1992.

The old town hall was completely renovated in 2015–2016 and is still used daily for normal administrative services: driving licences, passports or applications are stamped in the large hall, while couples are married in the neighbouring room. And it is all open to the public.

Address Rue du Curé / Pastoorstraat 2, 1190 Brussels (Forest / Vorst), +32 (0)2 3702211 | **Getting there** Tram 32, 82 or 97, or bus 50 or 54 to Forest Centre | **Hours** Mon – Thu 8.30am – 12.45pm, Fri 8.30 – 11.45am, in addition Wed 1.45 – 3.45pm, Thu 5 – 6.45pm | **Tip** The former brewery Wielemans-Ceuppens at Avenue van Volxem 354, a work of art in its own right, is today the home of Wiels, a centre for contemporary art, which presents international and Belgian avant-garde (www.wiels.org).

106__ Train World

A beguiling journey through the world of the railway

The Belgian king did the honours himself on 24 September, 2015, visiting the historic 1887 train station in the neighbourhood of Schaerbeek. The occasion was the inauguration of Train World, a railway museum the like of which can't be found anywhere else in the whole of Europe.

Belgium is particularly proud of its railway tradition. After all, one of the first passenger trains on the European continent puffed its way between Brussels and Mechelen on 5 May, 1835. In fact, Schaerbeek, the only completely preserved station in Brussels with impressive 19th-century architecture and still in full operation across many of its platforms, was a stop on the Belgian railway network's first route.

Part of the station, with its imposing, Flemish Renaissance-style foyer, belongs to the 8,000-square-metre museum landscape. It also includes, alongside an outdoor area right up to the tracks, four large and interlinked industrial halls with various floors. You can look out onto the tracks of the station and also towards the city from bridges across the floors. There are 22 historic locomotives and carriages to be admired in the newly built halls, all of them originals: the first steam train built in Belgium 'Le Belge' from 1835, the 'Pays de Waes' from 1844, the aerodynamic type-12 steam locomotive and contemporary high-speed trains. There are also dozens of carriages to be seen, including luxurious 1st-class compartments and the royal Pullman carriage. On top of this, there is also an original railway bridge from the 19th century, a track bed under transparent, walk-on covers, signals, a signal box and station clocks of all kinds. The interactive Train World holds many surprises for the visitor. The concept was developed by the comic author and artist François Schuiten, born in Brussels in 1956, on behalf of the National Railway Company of Belgium SNCB.

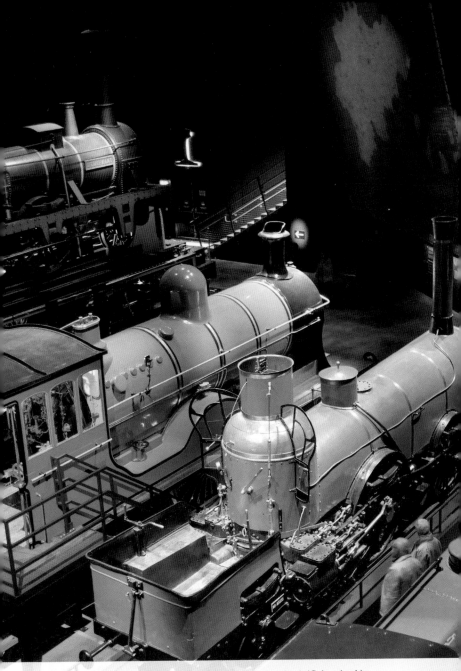

Address Place Princesse Elisabeth 5, 1030 Brussels (Schaerbeek/Schaarbeek), +32 (0)2 2247498 | Getting there Tram 7 or 92 or bus 58 or 59 to Schaerbeek | Hours Tue–Sun 10am–5pm (last tickets at 3.30pm) | Tip Driving along Rue Royale you will approach the massive church Sainte-Marie of Schaerbeek with its huge dome.

107__The Triumvirate
Manneken, Jeanneke *and* Zinneke Pis

The Brussels locals occasionally have a really crude sense of humour. This is certainly the impression you get when you contemplate the triumvirate of Brussels statues that very publicly satisfy their most natural of needs.

The newest, *Zinneke Pis*, is a street dog with its leg lifted, a mongrel, in Brussels dialect a Zinneke. It was created by the Belgian sculptor Tom Frantzen and was installed in 1998. The naked girl by the name Jeanneke has been crouching down and peeing in a niche in Impasse de la Fidélité since 1987. The 55.5-centimetre-tall statue of *Petit Julien*, also called *ketje* and known around the world as *Manneken Pis*, has, on the other hand, been weeing (drinking) water into a fountain for nearly 400 years. The original of the statue by Jérome Duquesnoy the Elder (1570–1641), the most famous sculptor in Brussels of his time, is from the year 1619.

There are numerous stories about the meaning of the little peeing boy. The most popular suggests he extinguished a bomb on the neighbouring Grand-Place with a well-directed jet of 'water'. But this explanation can be easily pooh-poohed, as the first documented mention of a urinating statue of a boy is from as early as 1451. Ketje, the Brabant word for 'little boy', has been a symbolic figure for Brussels, and a tourist attraction, for 600 years. Millions of people from all around the world have visited him, gaped and laughed at him. Many have also been disappointed because they had expected a much bigger figure.

The name Ketje provides what is possibly the best explanation of what the statue is all about. Ketje, the urchin, is cheeky, someone who isn't afraid to show some audacity: public peeing as a symbol of a rebellious self-confidence. *Zinneke Pis* also fits into this tradition. And the locals like to describe themselves as Zinneke: cheeky, headstrong, but intelligent mongrels.

Address *Zinneke Pis*: Rue des Chartreux / Kartuizersstraat 35, 1000 Brussels; *Jeanneke Pis*: Impasse de la Fidélité / Getrouwheidsgang 10–12, 1000 Brussels; *Manneken Pis*: Rue de l'Étuve / Stoofstraat, 1000 Brussels | Getting there Metro 3 or 4 to Beurs / Bourse | Hours Accessible 24 hours | Tip In every even year in spring the Zinneke parade takes place in the district around the Bourse and Place Saint-Géry, a colourful street party with various theatre and dance groups that celebrates the diversity of the city.

108__ Tropismes

One of the most beautiful bookshops in the world

These rooms have already been through a lot: at the end of the 19th century, Brussels' high society met here in the classy Café du Prince. Then the premises became a pub, with all of the fashionable bells and whistles of the time: high ceilings, columns, iron beams and stucco, wreaths of lianas and hops branches. Birds of prey and swans with spread wings adorn the pillars. The ceilings are decorated with seashells, and framed, oversized mirrors cleverly reflect the light. Here was the industrial decor of the time, set in a dramatic light by an unknown architect. A variety of tenants and a variety of activities followed.

The rooms were once a salon for orchestral music, a billiards saloon in the 1920s, then a cabaret and dancing bar again. After World War II there was a fencing club here. By the start of the 1960s, the jazz club Blue Note was housed in these rooms, and there, where the poetry and verse section is today, Jacques Brel sang on a small stage. Finally, it was a brasserie. From then on, things went downhill.

In 1984, the two book dealers Brigitte de Meeûs and Jacques Bauduin discovered these venerable, but completely run-down premises in the ritzy shopping arcade and opened their bookshop, which is today one of the most beautiful in Europe. The shop has 80,000 different books on offer – from literary classics to specialist volumes. Bookshelves and book tables are elegantly draped between pillars, stucco and mirrors. It is worthwhile going up to the mezzanine floor, which contains the art book section and allows a wonderful view of the hall of mirrors.

Tropismes, named after a work by the French author Nathalie Sarraute (1900–1999), is located in Galeries des Princes, part of the fascinating, 213-metre-long Royal Sankt-Hubertus arcades from 1847, built by the architect Jean-Pierre Cluysenaar (1811–1880) in the style of Florentine Renaissance.

Address Galerie des Princes/Prinsengalerij 11, 1000 Brussels, +32 (0)2 5128852, www.tropismes.com | **Getting there** Metro 1 or 5, or bus 38, 65, 66 or 71 to De Brouckère and Gare Centrale/Centraal Station | **Hours** Mon 11am–6.30pm, Tue–Thu 10am–6.30pm, Fri 10am–7.30pm, Sat 10.30am–7pm, Sun 1.30–6.30pm | **Tip** Galeries Saint-Hubert is right next to the restaurant hotspot around Rue des Bouchers. The restaurant De l'Ogenblik is worth checking out (Galeries des Princes 1).

109___The Vaartkapoen

The young sewer worker from Molenbeek

A manhole cover suddenly opens up and a young man grabs at the leg of a passing policeman. He trips and stumbles and stretches out his hands in front of him to protect himself, with a horrified face and a scream, before he crashes to the floor. A scene frozen in time, like a snapshot, full of dynamism and ambiguity, humorously staged by the renowned Brussels sculptor Tom Frantzen in 1985. The bronze sculpture *De Vaartkapoen*, which means something like 'sewer rogue', is in front of the municipal offices of the Communauté Française, the Parliament of the Federation Wallonia-Brussels, on the Brussels–Charleroi canal in the district of Molenbeek. The intention of the artist: the young man, the Vaartkapoen, suddenly appears from the underground sewage system, causes the policeman to fall and thus rebels against the authorities and its power. Any conclusions, according to the artist, are left to the viewer. But Frantzen also wants his sculpture to be understood as a reference to the comic illustrator Hergé, whom he admires, and his humour.

Molenbeek, which lies to the west of the old town of Brussels and is separated from it by a canal, is one of the biggest of the 19 municipalities in Brussels with around 100,000 inhabitants and historically has the highest proportion of immigrants in the city. These are mainly Moroccans and people from other north African countries, who came here in the 1960s. The streets and squares along the canal have a predominantly Muslim feel. The borough hit the international headlines after the terrorist attacks in Paris on 13 November, 2015 and in Brussels on 22 March, 2016: the terrorists' tracks led back to Molenbeek. The district, which is clearly difficult to control and thus to govern, is considered a breeding ground for Islamic terrorism in Europe and a centre of radical Islam in Belgium.

Address Place Sainctelette / Boulevard Léopold II, 1080 Brussels (Molenbeek) | **Getting there** Metro 1 or 5 to Comte de Flandre / Graaf van Vlaanderen, metro 2 or 6 to Yzer / Ijzer or tram 51 to Sainctelette | **Hours** Accessible 24 hours | **Tip** The sewage museum is worth taking a look at (Musée des Égouts, Pavillon d'Octroi, Porte d'Anderlecht).

110_ The Warehouse

Antiques by the pile

Brussels is famous for the large number of shops selling antiques of all kinds. The antiques district begins on Sablon and stretches via the two parallel streets Rue Haute and Rue Blaes towards Midi and the flea market on Place du Jeu de Balle. Most of the shops are specialised, either in one era or style, or in particular objects, lamps or furniture. Galerie des Minimes, however, is a little bit different. At first sight you get the impression of a completely haphazard and mammoth hotchpotch, as if someone had stuffed and piled as many diverse items of furniture and objects into a hall as possible, randomly and without thinking. When you enter the winding rooms, which extend over several half-storeys, you automatically begin to move more carefully, worried about knocking something over.

If you take a closer look, however, it becomes clear that small units, like individual rooms, are arranged out of the sofas, tables and cupboards. There is large and small furniture, for inside and out, fine wood with delicate inlays as well as clearly battered pieces, there are standard lamps and desk lamps, chandeliers of crystal or Murano glass, in between pictures in the most varied of styles, tapestries or stuffed ibexes, church pews next to swords and old pistols, marble pillars and bronze statues. There is probably even an old aeroplane propeller somewhere – and there is some method to the madness. The general impression you are left with is of a huge omnium-gatherum, which is a rather rare thing in itself at such a size and range. Very few of the pieces are labelled with a fixed price, but they all certainly have one.

However, the time of snapping up big bargains on the antiques market is over. All the dealers are professionals now. They know what they've got and what it's worth. But of course, it can't do any harm to discuss the price and haggle a bit.

Address Galerie des Minimes, Rue des Minimes / Miniemenstraat 23, 1000 Brussels, +32 (0)2 5112825, www.galeriedesminimes.com | Getting there Tram 92 or 93 to Petit Sablon or bus 27, 48 or 95 to Grand Sablon | Hours Daily 10am–6pm | Tip Brussels most well-known flea market takes place every day on Place du Jeu de Balle. From junk to art, from dirt cheap to high class, you'll find it all here.

111 Zero Point

From where the country is measured

Most people who visit Brussels Town Hall on Grand-Place and enter the quadratic courtyard, walk heedlessly over the cobblestones without noticing the special structure built into them. But on closer inspection, in the centre of the square, just in front of the fountain that embodies Belgium's two major rivers, the Meuse (Maas) and the Scheldt (L'Escaut), you will find a star-shaped structure embedded in the ground.

You could be forgiven for thinking it is a random decorative element, but far from it. This is a special feature that even the most dyed-in-the-wool locals don't know about and there is no indication or information plaque stating what the dark cobbled circle and star actually means. It is in fact Belgium's geographical zero point, from where all lengths, or rather distances, in the kingdom were measured – to Leuven, Dendermonde and Antwerp, as well as to Cologne, Aachen and Paris.

Brussels Town Hall, built between 1401 and 1421, is a late-Gothic masterpiece, in the so-called Brabantine Gothic style, intended to exemplify Brussels' economic and political power. The building is captivating, with its extraordinary, richly ornate exterior façade and delicate decorative sculptures. And then there is the huge belfry that towers above everything else. The artfully designed bell tower, the tallest in Belgium at 96 metres high, was built in 1455 and is crowned by Saint Michael, the patron saint of Brussels, in the form of a weather vane. Most important was that the Brussels belfry should be taller than that of Bruges and demonstrate the self-confidence of Brussels' citizens. The Town Hall almost burned to the ground during the bombardment of the Grand-Place by the French in 1695, but it was reconstructed immediately after this catastrophe and, with some alterations and extensions, appeared in its current splendid form.

Address Hôtel de Ville / Stadhuis, Grand-Place / Grote Markt, 1000 Brussels | Getting there Metro 1 or 5 to Gare Centrale / Centraal Station or metro 3 or 4 or tram 31 or 32 to Bourse / Beurs | Hours The courtyard can be visited at any time, but the Town Hall can only be viewed with a guided tour: Tue & Wed 2.30–4pm, Sun 10am–12.15pm | Tip Inside the Town Hall, especially in the council chamber and in the jury room, you can admire the most precious Brussels tapestries from the 16th, 17th and 18th centuries.

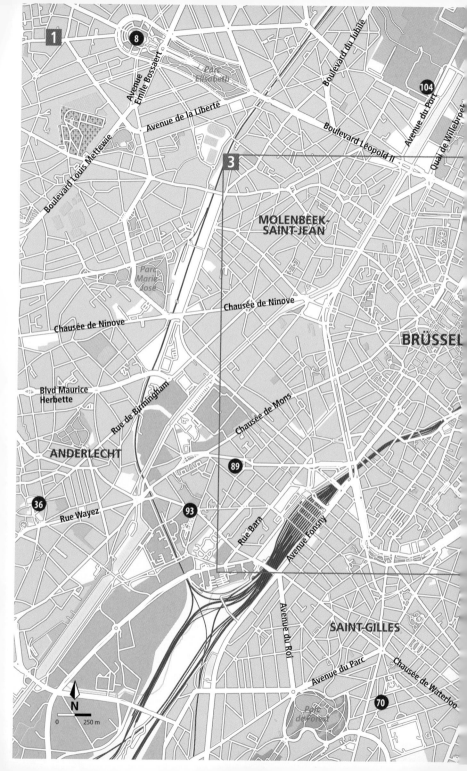

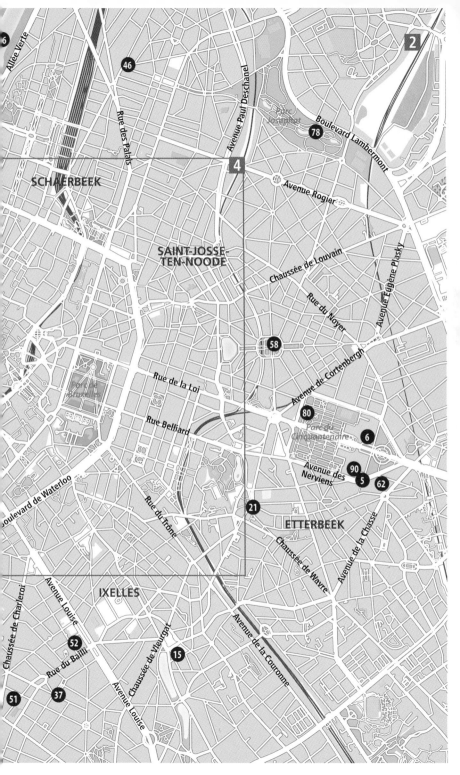

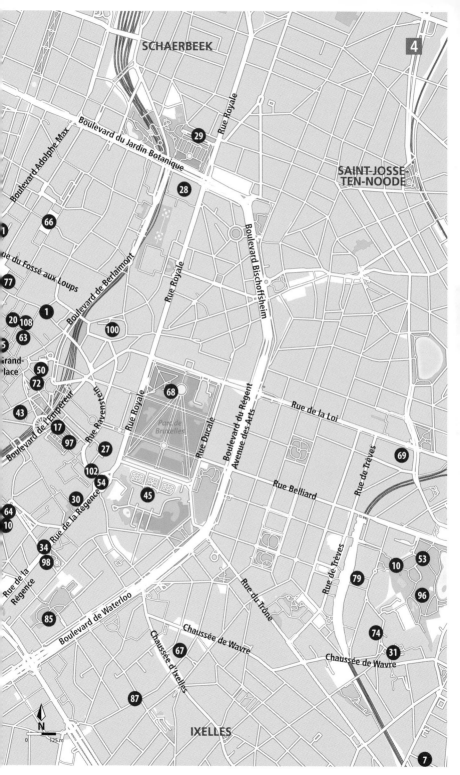

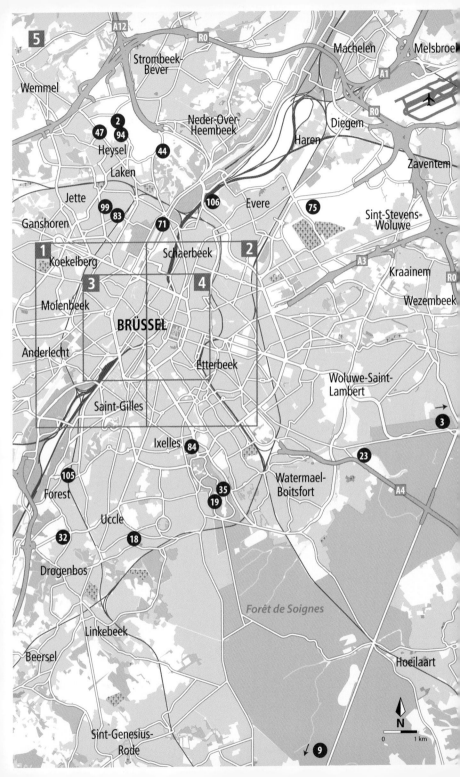

Dirk Engelhardt
**111 PLACES IN BARCELONA
THAT YOU MUST NOT MISS**
ISBN 978-3-95451-353-6

Rüdiger Liedtke
**111 PLACES ON MALLORCA
THAT YOU SHOULDN'T MISS**
ISBN 978-3-95451-281-2

Marcus X. Schmid
**111 PLACES IN ISTANBUL
THAT YOU MUST NOT MISS**
ISBN 978-3-95451-423-6

Jo-Anne Elikann
**111 PLACES IN NEW YORK
THAT YOU MUST NOT MISS**
ISBN 978-3-95451-052-8

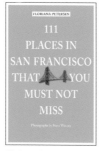

Floriana Petersen, Steve Werney
**111 PLACES IN SAN
FRANCISCO THAT YOU
MUST NOT MISS**
ISBN 978-3-95451-609-4

Christiane Bröcker,
Babette Schröder
**111 PLACES IN STOCKHOLM
THAT YOU MUST NOT MISS**
ISBN 978-3-95451-459-5

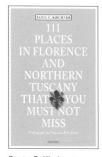

Beate C. Kirchner
**111 PLACES IN FLORENCE
AND NORTHERN TUSCANY
THAT YOU MUST NOT MISS**
ISBN 978-3-95451-613-1

Lucia Jay von Seldeneck,
Carolin Huder, Verena Eidel
**111 PLACES IN BERLIN
THAT YOU SHOULDN'T MISS**
ISBN 978-3-95451-208-9

Laurel Moglen, Julia Posey
**111 PLACES IN LOS ANGELES
THAT YOU SHOULDN'T MISS**
ISBN 978-3-95451-884-5

Michael Murphy, Sall Asher
**111 PLACES IN NEW ORLEANS
THAT YOU MUST NOT MISS**
ISBN 978-3-95451-645-2

Petra Sophia Zimmermann
**111 PLACES IN VERONA
AND LAKE GARDA THAT
YOU MUST NOT MISS**
ISBN 978-3-95451-611-7

Rüdiger Liedtke,
Laszlo Trankovits
**111 PLACES IN CAPE TOWN
THAT YOU MUST NOT MISS**
ISBN 978-3-95451-610-0

Gillian Tait
**111 PLACES IN EDINBURGH
THAT YOU SHOULDN'T MISS**
ISBN 978-3-95451-883-8

Rike Wolf
**111 PLACES IN HAMBURG
THAT YOU SHOULDN'T MISS**
ISBN 978-3-95451-234-8

Giulia Castelli Gattinara,
Mario Verin
**111 PLACES IN MILAN
THAT YOU MUST NOT MISS**
ISBN 978-3-95451-331-4

John Sykes
**111 PLACES IN LONDON
THAT YOU SHOULDN'T MISS**
ISBN 978-3-95451-346-8

Julian Treuherz,
Peter de Figueiredo
**111 PLACES IN LIVERPOOL
THAT YOU SHOULDN'T MISS**
ISBN 978-3-95451-769-5

Rüdiger Liedtke
**111 PLACES IN MUNICH
THAT YOU SHOULDN'T MISS**
ISBN 978-3-95451-222-5

Matěj Černý, Marie Peřinová
**111 PLACES IN PRAGUE
THAT YOU SHOULDN'T MISS**
ISBN 978-3-7408-0144-1

Sybil Canac, Renée Grimaud,
Katia Thomas
**111 PLACES IN PARIS THAT
YOU SHOULDN'T MISS**
ISBN 978-3-7408-0159-5

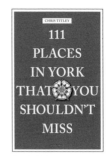

Chris Titley
**111 PLACES IN YORK THAT
YOU SHOULDN'T MISS**
ISBN 978-3-95451-768-8

Kathrin Bielfeldt,
Raymond Wong, Jürgen Bürger
**111 PLACES IN HONG KONG
THAT YOU SHOULDN'T MISS**
ISBN 978-3-95451-936-1

Justin Postlethwaite
**111 PLACES IN BATH THAT
YOU SHOULDN'T MISS**
ISBN 978-3-7408-0146-5

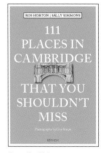

Rosalind Horton,
Sally Simmons, Guy Snape
**111 PLACES IN CAMBRIDGE
THAT YOU SHOULDN'T MISS**
ISBN 978-3-7408-0147-2

Frank McNally
**111 PLACES IN DUBLIN
THAT YOU SHOULDN'T MISS**
ISBN 978-3-95451-649-0

Gerd Wolfgang Sievers
**111 PLACES IN VENICE
THAT YOU MUST NOT MISS**
ISBN 978-3-95451-460-1

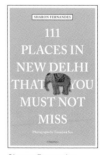

Sharon Fernandes
**111 PLACES IN NEW DELHI
THAT YOU MUST NOT MISS**
ISBN 978-3-95451-648-3

The authors

Kay Walter is a journalist who has lived in Brussels for many years, where he has made numerous films about the city and its people. He loves the refined chaos of Brussels, and he especially appreciates the cuisine and the beer. He strives to find out what lies behind the shining façades along the city streets.

Rüdiger Liedtke, author and journalist, has written four other books in the 111 series about Munich and Mallorca.